"*Anxiety Happens* is a gem of a book. It reads like a gentle journey with a wise and caring guide. The highly expert authors guide you every step of the way, as you develop the willingness, self-compassion, and wisdom needed to embrace the fullness of a life well lived. It's just excellent."

—**Dennis Tirch, PhD**, author of
The Compassionate-Mind Guide
to Overcoming Anxiety

"John and Georg have done it again: this is now their third superb book for radically transforming the way we respond to anxiety. In fifty-two bite-sized chapters, they'll show you a wide variety of simple yet powerful ways to powerfully change your relationship with fear, anxiety, and insecurity in all their different forms. You'll learn not just how to disarm anxiety, but how to actively utilize it to build a rich and meaningful life. If you want to get past your blocks and barriers, develop a deep sense of inner security, and do those important things that really scare you—this is the book for you!"

—**Russ Harris**, author of
The Happiness Trap

Anxiety Happens

52 WAYS TO FIND PEACE *of* MIND

JOHN P. FORSYTH, PhD
GEORG H. EIFERT, PhD

New Harbinger Publications, Inc.

Publisher's Note

This publication is designed to provide accurate and authoritative information in regard to the subject matter covered. It is sold with the understanding that the publisher is not engaged in rendering psychological, financial, legal, or other professional services. If expert assistance or counseling is needed, the services of a competent professional should be sought.

Distributed in Canada by Raincoast Books

Copyright © 2018 by John P. Forsyth and Georg H. Eifert
New Harbinger Publications, Inc.
5674 Shattuck Avenue
Oakland, CA 94609
www.newharbinger.com

Cover design by Amy Shoup; Acquired by Catharine Meyers; Edited by Kristi Hein

---

Library of Congress Cataloging-in-Publication Data

Names: Forsyth, John P., 1965- author. | Eifert, Georg H., 1952- author.
Title: Anxiety happens : 52 ways to find peace of mind / John P. Forsyth, PhD, and Georg H. Eifert, PhD.
Description: Oakland, CA : New Harbinger Publications, Inc., [2018]
Identifiers: LCCN 2017044311 (print) | LCCN 2017050888 (ebook) | ISBN 9781684031115 (PDF e-book) | ISBN 9781684031122 (ePub) | ISBN 9781684031108 (pbk. : alk. paper)
Subjects: LCSH: Anxiety--Treatment--Popular works. | Meditation--Therapeutic use.
Classification: LCC RC531 (ebook) | LCC RC531 .F669 2018 (print) | DDC 616.85/2206--dc23
LC record available at https://lccn.loc.gov/2017044311

20   19   18

10   9   8   7   6   5   4   3   2

For my wife, Jamie: your enduring love and support have turned darkness into light and have made all things possible. I love you! And for the many people who struggle with anxiety and fear: this book is a testament to your courage, strength, and basic goodness.

—JPF

For my wife, Diana: I am grateful and truly blessed that we can share our paths toward fulfillment with love, humor, and joy—we know that all possibilities are within us. And for my teachers, different ones at different times: without your inspiration I would not be where I am today.

—GHE

Contents

Acknowledgments

The seeds of this book were planted several years ago when Catharine Myers—our associate publisher at New Harbinger and a longtime friend—encouraged us to share our collective wisdom, teachings, and exercises that over the years we've found to be of enormous benefit to so many people who struggle with anxiety. Catherine has supported us tirelessly through many writing projects for well over a decade, including inspiring us to write this book. We deeply appreciate her friendship and wise counsel, along with her creative spirit and editorial skills. Thank you!

We would also like to thank our copy editor, Kristi Hein, for her tireless and masterful editing. The book you have in your hands is better than it was because of Kristi's gentle touch and astute suggestions during the editing process.

And finally, we would like to thank you, the reader, for having enough faith in us to pick up this book and see what it may offer you. Know that you are not walking alone and you have everything you need to thrive when anxiety happens. We wish you much peace and joy on your life journey!

Introduction

We live in an age of anxiety. It's an experience shared by millions of people on this planet. You may know what it's like. You feel it. You think it. You may confront it from the moment you wake up until you go to sleep at night. Even then, sleep may offer no comfort.

There's no escaping this simple truth. Anxiety has been with us for as long as we know. Our ancestors needed it to survive. We need it too. But in our modern industrialized world, few of us are facing down predators on a daily basis. Still, many experience anxiety and fear daily, and, in a way, it can feel like being followed by a hungry lion wherever you go. Over time, anxiety can strip away your passion and zest for life. And it can literally take over your life and *become* your life. It's bad enough just to have anxiety. But when it begins to rob you of your freedom, you have a *problem* with anxiety. Yet it doesn't have to be this way.

This little book offers fifty-two ways to break free from the snares, the traps, and all the false hopes and promises that anxiety and fear set for you. Like a child throwing a tantrum, anxiety forces itself into our awareness and can deplete our energy, resources, and resolve. It screams, *"Pay attention to me or else!"* It makes it seem like your life is at stake. But the biggest "or else" message is this: "You won't be happy, so long as you feel anxious or afraid." This is a natural setup for endless struggle. Anxiety is no longer an emotion that can be felt and experienced. Anxiety is now a problem that must be overcome before you can have the kind of life you so desperately want. Yet it doesn't have to be this way either.

The Struggle Is Costly

Ancient wisdom and modern science teach us that anxiety and fear are two of many unpleasant emotions that all human beings will experience as long as they're alive. In fact, you wouldn't be reading this book without them. But the struggle with anxiety is different. It is the source of great hardship and pain—and it is mostly unnecessary. This is important to understand.

Often, when anxiety and fear show up, we see them as the enemy. We harden, shut down, and withdraw. Naturally, then, we want to struggle to bury them, fight them, or run away from them. Meanwhile, the clock is ticking. Moments spent struggling to feel less anxious or afraid add up, and the cumulative effort starts to take its toll. If you allow this to go unchecked, you may find yourself one day looking back and facing the worst kind of pain—the pain of missed opportunities and regrets.

Anxiety in and of itself, without the struggle, can be useful in many ways. Our ancestors needed it to stay safe and alive. We need it in the modern-day world too.

Sometimes anxiety is a warning call, telling us that something is wrong or even harmful or dangerous. It may even give you a nudge to accomplish goals. Or it may alert you to something amiss in your life. Maybe you're off course and far from the life you wish to lead. Anxiety will show up then too. Anxiety may also be a sign that something is so important to you that you care intensely about it. So intensely, in fact, that you fear losing it.

What you don't need is the constant struggle with anxiety. Paradoxically, the more you try to get rid of anxiety, the more it gains a hold on you. It often increases over time. Learning to *let go of the struggle* is a powerful antidote to the misery caused by endless unsuccessful struggles with your emotional pain.

The Freedom to Create Your Best Life

Since the dawn of time, millions of people all over the world have felt the self-limiting blows of crushing anxiety and fear. We certainly have too. Many have also found enormous grace and healing by walking themselves through the material we're about to share with you. And their lives are better for it. This can happen for you too.

This book offers you hope and a way into the life you want, one in which you're not held back by your struggles with anxiety. This new approach is based on several streams of solid research, our own and that of others, spanning emotion science (that is, work showing that suppression and control of thoughts and feelings makes them worse), mindfulness-based interventions such as acceptance and commitment therapy (ACT), and contemporary research supporting positive life changes, human thriving, and psychological health and wellness. We won't be covering the science in this book—this is not the place for that. Rather, we are offering you a set of tested strategies that will help you tip the scales back to where anxiety becomes just a normal part of living fully. But this is hard to do unless you're willing to look at things differently.

There is a space between you and what you think and feel—a moment in time when you can choose how to respond and what you will do. In this space, you can choose to relate differently with your anxious mind and body—and your life. You can learn to let go of the struggle and start moving in directions in which you want your life to go. This is the way to create genuine happiness, peace of mind, and a wholehearted life. This book aims to start you on this journey.

Some ideas and teachings in this book may seem odd, backward, even strange to you. But if you stick with them, you'll gain freedom from suffering and the turmoil that anxiety creates in your life. You'll learn how to transform your relationship with anxiety. No longer tormented by it. No longer a slave to it. You'll learn to tap into your inner strength and courage to let anxiety be without getting knocked around by it. Then, and only then, will you be free to do what you really care about.

We invite you to dive into this book with an open mind and a willingness to try something new, opposite, and different from what you've done before. As you do, be mindful that we're not asking you to like what you think or feel. Nobody likes anxiety or fear. Nor will we ask you to condone past wrongs committed against you. What we'll teach you is how to *move beyond anxiety and fear* and create the optimal conditions for your own genuine happiness and *peace of mind*. This is something you can do.

Use This Book Wisely

This book will teach you fifty-two ways to stop running from your anxiety, fears, and worries and instead spend more time creating the life you want to live. To benefit, you don't need to believe what we say. You don't even need to understand all of it.

The simple, short, and powerful exercises in this book offer you new experiences, skills, and ways of approaching anxiety *and* your life. Do the exercises in a quiet place where you feel comfortable and distraction is limited. Let's call this your peaceful place, your safe refuge. Simply read the instructions twice and follow them as best as you can.

We guarantee that your mind will throw many arguments at you as to why this or that sounds impossible, is too difficult, or doesn't make any sense. When such thoughts show up, thank your mind for each of them. Then move on. There's no need to argue with your mind. Don't get stuck trying to convince yourself of anything.

The only thing we ask is that you stay open. Do the exercises and check out whether, over time, they start working for you. You have little to lose and much to gain by approaching your anxiety problems in a radically different way. We'll show you that way.

Of course, you don't have to keep on doing *all* the exercises forever. The whole point of the exercises is to teach you a new way of navigating life's ups and downs so that you can live in alignment with what matters to you. Make a note of the exercises that work best for you, and then keep on practicing those! After a while they will become a habit. It's also a good idea to go back and reread chapters that deal with issues you continue to struggle with.

Keep in mind that this book offers a journey of change, growth, and self-discovery. To make a real difference in your life, you'll need to start doing something new and unlike anything you've done before. That's what this book offers you—the hope of a new life even with anxiety. When you wholeheartedly and genuinely work with this book, it will work for you. You'll find that you're freer to exercise your capacity to create your own destiny without anxiety limiting you. That much we know from our own research and experience. So let's get started.

1 LIVE Your Life

All of us wish to be genuinely happy and to thrive. But this isn't easy to do. Life will inevitably offer obstacles, problems, and pain. No one can escape this simple truth. But this doesn't mean you have to be miserable. It doesn't mean that you have to live in fear.

Anxiety happens. It's not a choice. But you can live your life without anxiety controlling you. This doesn't mean that you'll never feel any painful emotions again. You will. We will. Every person on this planet will. But feeling these emotions when you feel them doesn't mean that you have to suffer.

Emotions happen. We have little control over them. But you can control how you respond to your emotional life. Anxiety doesn't have to control you. It is you who can decide whether anxiety and fear control you or not. You can learn to feel whatever you feel and think whatever you think *and* go forward to create the kind of life you wish to live. This is the path to unlocking your inner power to control your life and create genuine happiness.

You can create the conditions for your genuine happiness and peace of mind. You don't have to remain stuck in anxiety and fear, or mired down in the difficulties that life offers. The trick is learning to live well when life is hard and unkind. This is the heart of the LIVE approach in this book:

Letting go. You've probably heard it said that "what you resist, persists." And what you resist will amplify your pain and suffering while draining your energy and robbing you of your freedom. The way out of this cycle is to learn to let go of the struggle with what your mind and body offer you. In this way, you free up your precious energy and resources to do what you really care about and LIVE without fear controlling you.

Inviting. Nobody chooses anxiety. But you can choose how you relate with it. Instead of resisting, you learn to open up to what you're experiencing anyway. You get curious. You learn to welcome all aspects of you—everything that your mind, body, and emotional life dish out. You watch and welcome your experiences with kindness and compassion—with love. Stepping back and allowing will help you find peace and joy, even in difficulty, and LIVE your best life.

Valuing. Without a clear sense of direction, our choices in life can lead us astray—or worse, toward dead ends. To really LIVE, you'll need to know what you wish to LIVE for. You'll need to clarify what really matters to you—your values—and then make wise choices that support the kind of person you wish to be and the kind of life you wish to lead.

Engaging. No matter how you cut it, your life is created by what you spend your time doing. To do more of what you really desire in life, you'll need to set intentions that are in line with what matters to you and then take action—in short, you'll need to do something with your mouth, hands, and feet (that is, speaking, creating, stepping in a direction). This is how you LIVE out your important values. As you engage your values and your life, you'll be armed with a new set of skills from this book to help you move with any challenges that show up along the way and to LIVE wholeheartedly.

The following brief exercise will give you a small taste of the LIVE approach.

WHAT IT MEANS TO LIVE

- Recall a recent time when you found yourself running late or stuck waiting in traffic or a store checkout line. Bring the scene to life as we walk you through each piece of LIVE.

- Letting go—Let go of your old struggle with anxiety and fruitless attempts to control what you're experiencing in your mind and body.

- **Inviting**—Open up and notice the thoughts and feelings you're having as you sit or stand there, stuck. Notice the judgment, complaining, huffing and puffing under your breath, and expletives. Notice the effect this is having on your body. Do you feel tension, anger, anxiety, stress, frustration, even fear? See if you can simply watch all this activity—step back and notice it for what it is, with some kindness and friendliness. There's nothing to do except to be right where you are.

- **Valuing**—Step back further, as if watching yourself, and ask what you want to be about right now, as a person, in this situation. See if you can connect with what matters to you, which may include the reason you're out and about in the first place. You have somewhere you want to go, something you want to do.

- **Engaging**—Imagine yourself doing something other than getting all worked up about being delayed, stuck, and waiting. What would you do? What do you want to be about as a person? What would that look like right now? Whatever it is, see yourself using your mouth, hands, and feet to do something that reflects what you want to be about in this situation—what you value and care about.

If this exercise didn't flow easily for you, don't worry. The point is to see how struggle and suffering can show up in common, everyday situations and how we can learn to let go, open up, connect with what matters, and LIVE. As you read on, you'll learn how to master the skills inside the LIVE approach and be able to use them with anxiety or in other challenging areas of your life.

2 Find Connection

Many people suffering with anxiety feel utterly alone. You may feel that way too. You may think that nobody could possibly understand what it's like to feel as bad as you feel. But there are countless people all over the world who share your fears and your struggles. Consider how many people that might be.

People with anxiety problems live in every town, state, and country. Being young or old, rich or poor, offers no protection. Having a college degree or social status offers little comfort either. In fact, anxiety ranks among the most common of all forms of human suffering that we know of, affecting about one-third of the population at some point in their lifetimes. That's about one hundred million people in the United States alone.

To bring the numbers home, imagine that one day everyone who struggles with anxiety decides to wear something red. If that were so, then you'd be hard-pressed to go about your day without seeing someone wearing red. If you asked one of these people how she was doing, the person may say "Fine," but inside you know the heart of it. You know that that person also suffers as you suffer. And in that moment you'd know that you're no longer alone.

But this book isn't about faceless people and statistics. It's about *you* and your freedom, and helping you to show up in your life, fully and without defenses. We'll start with an exercise that will teach you how to observe your experience just as it is. We focus on the breath because it's always with you, and it can be your refuge, guiding you back to the present moment—the place you need to fully inhabit if you want to make a difference in your life. Just read the instructions a few times first and then do the exercise on your own as best you can. Allow yourself five to ten minutes; set a timer if that helps.

CENTERED BREATHING

- Place one hand on your chest and the other on your belly. Allow your eyes to close gently, and get centered right where you are.

- Bring your attention to the rising and falling of your chest and belly. Notice the movement of your hands as you breathe in and out through your nose. Notice each inhale and slow exhale.

- Get curious about your experience. You may shift your awareness from the movement of your hands on your chest and belly to the sensations of warmth or coolness as you breathe in and out through your nose. Just breathe naturally and notice. Simply allow yourself to be here, now, with your breath.

- If thoughts or anything else distracts you, notice that and then gently bring your awareness back to the breath. Do this gently and as often as necessary.

- End this practice by setting an intention to come back to your centered breath as often as needed during your day. Set a timer on your phone or device as a reminder to check in with your breath and the present moment.

Practice this *Centered Breathing* exercise as often as you can. It's a powerful skill and antidote to the suffering that the mind and body can create around anxiety and fear. With each practice, you're developing your capacity to observe and be present with your experiences. This will help you create the necessary space to consider what really matters to you in this life.

3   Creating Space

Anxiety and fear will make you contract and will pull you into dark places far from the life you wish to lead. As you get smaller, so too will your life. That needs to change, because life is asking you to stretch your wings, open, and become the person you wish to be. So to counter the natural tendency to close and withdraw when anxiety strikes, you'll need to learn how to open and expand your awareness, right where you are.

The next exercise will help you learn to do just that. The aim is not to be open and expansive all the time—that's unrealistic—but to give you the skills to create inner space to acknowledge and make room for the experiences you're having anyway, as often as you need to. This is important so that you can show up to your life and live it. It's also important when anxiety and other unpleasant thoughts and emotions try to pull you into dark places, including the past that once was or a future that is yet to be.

There's no right or wrong way to do this exercise, or any of the others in this book, except for one directive: don't use them to fight your experience. Fighting will get you nowhere. Instead, set the intention to be here and now with whatever is happening anyway. Open up to your experience. Get curious about you and what's happening right now.

CREATING SPACE WITHIN

Get into a comfortable sitting position where you won't be disturbed for five to ten minutes. Read through the instructions a few times; then close your eyes and begin the practice. If you'd rather keep your eyes slightly open, that's okay, but it's best to focus on a spot—say, on the floor just in front of you—so you don't get too distracted.

- Allow your eyes to close gently. Take a couple of gentle breaths—in and out—and notice the sound and feel of your own breath as you breathe.

- Now turn your attention to being just where you are. Allow your awareness to drift to the world around you—what do you notice?

- Next, allow your awareness to drift inside of you. Gently acknowledge any physical sensations in your body. Do the same for any thoughts, and notice how they may change or shift from moment to moment.

- With each inhale, imagine that you're creating more and more space for any thoughts or sensations in your body, more space within you for you to be you, right here where you are.

- Continue breathing. Continue expanding until you experience a sense of spaciousness within you.

- Then, when you're ready, gradually widen your attention to take in the sounds around you, and slowly open your eyes with the intention to bring this centered awareness to the many moments to come in your day.

We encourage you to practice this *Creating Space Within* exercise daily. Find a time and place that's right for you. It will help you make room for you to show up and do what you care about, even if your mind and body offer you unpleasant stuff now and then.

4 Live with Intention

Most of us are creatures of habit. We run about our day on autopilot, without conscious awareness of what we're doing. If we allow this to go unchecked, we can quickly end up feeling cut off and disconnected from our lives and our hearts. Anxiety and fear are two powerful emotions that trigger this automatic, reactive way of being. Like a bully, they push many people into places they'd rather not go. But this isn't inevitable.

There is a space between you and the anxiety and fear where you can choose something new. In that space, you can learn to become more purposeful, less automatic. You can harness your capacity to follow your heart. To do that, you'll need to become clear about what you want to be about. You need to know your intentions for the kind of life you wish to lead. Only then can you consciously make commitments to act in ways that honor your intentions. In short, where your intentions go, your attention and energy will follow.

Let's pause for a moment and sink into what that might mean. When you commit to doing something new, what possibilities lie ahead for you? Do you even know? Have you taken time to consider what your life could become? The next brief exercise will help you get in touch with that.

HEARTFELT INTENTIONS

- Get into a comfortable sitting position where you won't be disturbed for five to ten minutes. You may also find it helpful to have a piece of paper and pen or pencil handy.

- Close your eyes and take a moment to center yourself. With each centering breath, let your awareness settle more deeply into the space around your heart. This is a place full of enormous wisdom—it knows what's right for you.

- As you settle into that heart space, ask yourself: Why are you here, reading this book? What do you want to be about in this life? What are your intentions going forward? Connect with the kind of life you wish to lead.

- Then sit quietly and listen to your heart for the answers. One by one they will come. Maybe it's just a whisper, or even a word or two. Whatever it is, connect with your inner wisdom about you and what you want to be about in this lifetime.

- When you're ready, slowly open your eyes. These are your intentions. If you like, you can also jot down your answers.

- Before ending this exercise, review your heartfelt intentions. Bring them to mind as clearly as you can, and if you've written them down, read them slowly. As you review, feel free to add any new intentions that might come to you. And then make a commitment to yourself to honor your intentions by doing the exercises in this book, even if they're hard to do at times.

- If you've written down your intentions, you can finish this exercise by signing your name at the bottom of your list. Your signature represents your commitment to do what you can to bring your intentions to life. Keep this list close by as you work with the material in this book.

Change can be scary and liberating at the same time. It involves some risk. Yet the risk of doing more of the same ought to be more frightening, for it has gotten you to this place. To get something new, you'll need to do something

new. It's that simple. And it starts with making a commitment, guided by your intentions, to change the way you do
things. When you start looking at your life and your anxiety
differently, you have much to gain and nothing to lose.

5   Release the Fear

Fear and anxiety are two unpleasant emotions that can be healthy and adaptive. They propel us into action. Their purpose is to keep us alive and out of trouble. That's it!

Anxiety and fear also come in many shapes and guises. You may experience the powerful rush of panic, along with intense bodily changes (like a racing heart), feelings of terror, and thoughts of impending doom. These panic attacks may seem to come out of the blue, or they may be triggered by specific situations (such as in social settings, in a crowded store, on an airplane, at certain heights).

You may be haunted by memories of traumatic experiences you once endured. Or you may find yourself caught in a cycle of unwelcome obsessive thoughts and ritualistic acts like checking, counting, or handwashing. But no matter what you do, you get only a brief honeymoon from the distress and fear. You may also worry day in and day out about all sorts of things (past, future, daily hassles) without resolution.

You may think that some of these descriptions sound like what you're dealing with. You may even go on to think that you have an anxiety disorder of some kind. But here, we'd like to issue a word of caution.

Anxiety and fear are emotions, not disorders. Every single living human being on this planet experiences both emotions at some points in life. Some may even experience dis-*ease*—meaning unease—around anxiety and fear, but that alone isn't a disorder. Medical and psychiatric professionals use labels to describe different forms of human suffering and dis-*ease*, but the labels are not you. Human suffering itself is not a disorder.

Diagnostic labels are just words. So don't cling to them, and don't identify with them. Let them go, because they're limiting. Focus instead on expanding your life in healthy ways.

Your experience doesn't have to match the features of one or more anxiety disorders to make you feel the need to get your life back on track. This is true even if you also tend to have other unpleasant feelings, like depression or anger, when you're anxious.

What really matters is how you answer this basic question: Are anxiety and fear a major problem in my life? If you answered yes, you're in very good company. The next important step is for you to identify how anxiety has become such a huge issue in your life.

Most people answer by pointing to the anxiety itself. Some point to the fact that they're feeling it. Others focus on having too much of it. Some also focus on how intense and unpleasant it is. We know that intense anxiety is very unpleasant and can be overwhelming at times. But take a step back for a moment and ask yourself: Is having too much anxiety really the heart of the problem? Let's look at what makes anxiety a problem for you.

WHAT'S THE PROBLEM?

Find a place where you can reflect and won't be disturbed. Then take a moment to really consider the following questions. Clarify your thoughts and answers to each question as openly and honestly as you know how. If you like, you can jot down your answers on a piece of paper.

With your anxieties and fears in mind, ask yourself:

- What have I been struggling with? (or) What are the most interfering and life-restricting aspects of my problems with anxiety?

Once you have an answer, ask yourself this:

- How exactly does anxiety become a problem in my life?

Facing these questions squarely is the key to making changes that will move you in directions that are truly important to you. The next chapter will take you more deeply into the heart of the struggle with anxiety and its toll on your life. This step is necessary to forge a new path and move in new directions.

6 Exploring the Costs

Deep down you already know that your best efforts to control or manage anxieties and fears haven't worked as you've hoped they would. Even worse, your struggle with anxiety has cost you. Maybe you've experienced broken and strained relationships, poor health and sickness, excessive stress, difficulties at school or work, poor concentration, or problems with alcohol or other substances. Or, in a more general way, you may feel like you've lost your freedom. Do you feel stuck because anxiety seems to stand in the way?

Now—this very moment—is your time to take stock and look clearly at where you've been, what you've become, and where you want to go. It's time to face the costs of waiting and struggling with your anxiety obstacles. It's time for your life to begin—finally.

The next exercise will help you get a better sense of the price you pay each time you get caught in the struggle with anxiety. For each area listed, reflect on the impact that your struggles with anxiety have on your life. Be honest with yourself and be specific. What have you missed out on, or been unable to do, because of the struggle? Jot down a few thoughts for each area if you like. Look at the costs that fit your experience.

TAKING STOCK

1. *Interpersonal costs.* How has struggling with your anxiety and fears affected your relationships and social bonds? Have friendships changed or been lost? Are you unable to engage in your roles as a spouse, partner, or parent because of anxiety? Do you feel more isolated and alone?

2. *Career costs.* How has struggling with anxiety affected your career (for example, have you ever quit or been fired because of attempts to get a handle on your anxiety)? Has a boss or coworkers commented on your performance because of your anxiety-management efforts? Have anxiety problems led to unemployment, disability, or a need to rely on social services?

3. *Health costs.* How has managing your worry, anxiety, and fear affected your health? Do you tend to get sick often? Do you have difficulties falling asleep and staying asleep? Do you fixate and stew over anxiety and worry to the point of feeling physically sick? Do you avoid exercise because it might bring on anxiety? Do you spend quite a bit of time in

the doctor's office or emergency room because of anxiety?

4. *Energy costs.* How has the effort to manage your anxiety affected your energy levels? Do you pour mental energy into worry, stress, fretting over distractions, checking, and negative thinking? Does the struggle leave you feeling drained, discouraged, fatigued, frustrated, or worn out?

5. *Emotional costs.* Has trying to get a handle on anxiety cost you emotionally? Do you carry regrets and guilt because of what you have done or failed to do as a result of your anxiety struggles? What about shame, feeling as though you are broken? Do you feel down, depressed, prone to anger and irritability?

6. *Financial costs.* How much money have you spent on managing your anxieties and fears? Consider money you've spent on psychotherapy, medications, doctor's visits, self-help books, audio or video recordings, or seminars. What have been your costs in terms of lost wages or expenses related to missing important and enjoyable events (such as tickets that you ended up not using)?

7. *Costs to freedom.* How have your efforts to control worry, anxiety, and fears limited your ability to do what you enjoy and want to do? Can you shop, drive near and far, take a train or plane, or go for a walk in your neighborhood, the park, a mall, or a forest? Is your day arranged around avoiding feeling anxious, panicky, or afraid?

Answering these questions with honesty is a crucial first step in a new direction. It's important that you know, and allow yourself to feel, the real impact of your struggles despite all your efforts to change. It takes courage to face the costs squarely.

When people do this exercise, they often end up with a deeper awareness. They see, perhaps for the first time, how all the effort they've poured into managing and controlling anxiety hasn't really worked. More deeply, they become fully conscious of how the struggle itself has damaged their lives and continues to do so.

If you find yourself in a similar spot right now, don't despair. This is exactly how it should be. The point is not to feel bad or beat yourself up, but to empower you to take steps in a new direction from this point forward. You cannot change the past. But the future is yours to create.

7 The Struggle Trap

You likely opened this book with the hope of finding a better way to manage and control your anxiety so that you can get on with living your life the way you wish. This makes sense so long as you, just like so many people, continue to see your anxiety itself as the problem. But what if the very act of seeing anxiety as the problem *is* the problem? Our intention in this book is to help you connect with this possibility, however backward that may sound.

You don't have to trust us here, either. Go back to all the costs of anxiety management and control you explored in the previous chapter. Ask yourself which has cost you more—the presence of anxiety and fear, or the desperate effort to make it stop and avoid it altogether?

Research and years of wisdom teach us that the struggle itself is a trap, one that will ensnare you when you actively resist and avoid your own experience. This isn't the time to blame yourself for struggling. It's a very natural response to pain and difficulty. But the key question you must ask yourself is "Has it worked?" Or, more boldly, "Has the struggle itself created more problems than it has solved?"

The next exercise will help you discover for yourself if this is so.

IS THE STRUGGLE WORKING?

Think about every approach you've tried to manage and control your anxiety—each coping strategy, each method you use to avoid or reduce your anxiety and fear. If you like, you can write them down on a piece of paper or in your journal. Then reflect on the following three questions and answer each with a yes or no. Do so as openly and as honestly as you know how. Listen to your gut—it knows the truth of your experience.

1. Are my anxiety-management strategies working—meaning that I am less anxious and happier with my life? Think long-term.

2. Has being an anxiety manager moved me in directions I want my life to take?

3. Have my anxiety-management and anxiety-coping strategies cost me in the sense of time, missed opportunities, regrets? In short, have they gotten in the way of things I want to do, what I care about? If you need help in finding the answer, revisit the costs you identified in Chapter 6.

Many people answer the first two questions with a No, and the third one with a big YES. But that's exactly what we would expect. We know of no healthy way to eliminate anxiety and fear without significant costs. Your gut probably tells you as much. Your gut is right on!

The secret to your freedom is to let go of trying to manage anxiety, because the effort eats up your time, energy, and resources and gets in the way of what you want to do. You're already on this path now. But only you can decide to stop trying to fight against anxiety and fear. We hope that you will make this choice right now, if you haven't done so already.

8 Letting Go

When you look at anxiety as a problem, it will naturally require a solution. But what if the solutions you've tried are actually making things worse? Let that possibility sink in for a moment.

You've learned from previous chapters that all your attempts to fix your anxieties haven't solved anything. Each so-called solution—each attempt to stop or at least stem the tide of your anxieties—has left a deep mark on you.

The following metaphor will help you connect with the costs and tremendous strain involved in struggling with your anxieties. It also teaches a surprising way out of the struggle so that you can get on with living your life.

IT'S TIME TO DROP THE ROPE

It may seem like you've been fighting a tug-of-war, with a team of anxiety monsters pulling at the other end of the rope. You've got both hands firmly clenching the rope, and your feet are dug in, stuck in the same position. Back and forth it goes. Yet no matter how hard you've pulled to defeat them, they've always come back stronger, pulling harder.

And as this battle plays out, you're getting more and more worked up—your chest tightens, your breathing becomes shallow, your teeth are clenched, your face is red, with pearls of sweat welling up on your forehead, and you're gripping so hard your knuckles turn white. You're stuck in an endless and exhausting fight for your life, or so it seems.

Your options appear limited. Your mind may tell you to pull harder, try harder, or dig in more. Maybe your mind suggests that there's a better medication or a new coping strategy that'll give you the strength to win. Yet isn't all of this more of the same—old wine, new label?

Here's another possibility: you don't need to win this fight. Suppose you just decided to give up fighting and drop the rope. Think about that.

Notice what happens to your hands and feet. They're free, right? And you've regained some mental space and options that were impossible to even consider while you were in the middle of the battle. You're now able to use your mind, hands, and feet for something other than fighting anxiety.

To help you see how this might play out in your life, imagine that something or someone you care deeply about is on the sidelines next to the tug-of-war, watching and waiting for you to finish and the fight to end. Suppose it's your child waiting for a hug, or a friend wanting to spend time with you. Or perhaps it's a project, a vacation, or something spiritually uplifting. See if you can visualize that important thing in your life on the sidelines, just waiting…waiting for you to finish fighting. Would you just keep at it? Or would you drop the rope and give your time and energy to whatever or whomever was waiting for you?

Now, consider what happens when you drop the rope. The anxiety monsters haven't gone away just because you've stopped fighting. They're still there, taunting you with the rope, hoping that you take the bait and grab hold for another round. And you could certainly do that. Sometimes you will, mostly out of habit.

But the important thing is to notice when you've grabbed the rope, and make a choice to let go. Making this choice will give you the space and energy to attend to something you care about—important things in your life waiting on the sidelines.

Dropping the rope and ending the struggle creates an opening and room to do something else in your life. If you aren't consumed with reducing and controlling anxiety, avoiding the next panic attack, stemming the tide of another painful memory, or pushing away disturbing thoughts or "what-iffing" worries, then you create a window of opportunity. You create space to move toward the life you've put on hold. One of our clients captured this moment very well when he told us, *"When I drop the rope, I'm free."*

9 Flip the Switch

Why are so many people reluctant to drop the rope? Why do we keep struggling with anxiety and fear when it hasn't really worked well and has cost us so much? The answer has to do with what we've learned about control.

From a very young age, you've learned that control—doing something—works in the world around you. It's what helps you get your laundry done. It's what you do when taking out the garbage, driving your car, texting a friend. It's also helped keep you safe and alive, and it certainly helped keep our ancestors from being eaten by lions and tigers and bears. If something outside of you threatens your health and welfare, it makes sense to take action.

Because control works so well in the world around us, we naturally try to control—do something—to change what's going on inside us. The rub, though, is that control doesn't work as well when you apply it to the products of your mind and emotional life.

Why might this be? The next exercise will help you experience part of the answer.

THE TROUBLE WITH CONTROL

Start by getting into a comfortable position. When you're ready, do the following: make yourself as happy as you know how to be. Go ahead and try it now. Really work at it. But don't cheat by bringing to mind something that makes you happy. This isn't what we're asking of you. We want you to just flip the happiness switch and be super happy for the sake of it. Can you do it?

Now, try to make yourself feel really anxious or afraid. Do it without thinking of something really scary or painful. Try really hard. Just flip the anxiety switch. Can you do it?

If you're still not convinced about how impossible this really is, then you can go on to try one of the following:

- Make yourself fall madly in love—meaning genuine, deeply felt love—with the first new person you see.

- Using your willpower, go ahead and make your left leg numb, so numb in fact that if it were pricked with a sharp needle you wouldn't feel a thing.

- Pick a memory of something that happened to you last week, and then just delete it so that you're 100 percent sure that it's gone for good.

- Without covering your eyes, ears, or nose, stop seeing, hearing, and smelling.

We hope this brief exercise helps you discover that emotions, and many of our mental and bodily functions, have no on-off switch. Nobody has that switch. It's next to impossible for anyone to feel one way or another just because they want to.

Emotions just happen—they are part of your history that gets conjured up as you interact with your world. When you try to flip the "no more anxiety" switch, you'll activate every aspect of your nervous system that keeps you feeling anxious and afraid. And you'll do things that end up keeping you stuck and miserable. You'll get more of the very thing you don't want to feel and think.

10 Do the Opposite

Thoughts and feelings of anxiety and panic are unpleasant, intense, overwhelming at times, and even terrifying. But they're not the real enemy. The real enemy is rigid avoidance.

Avoidance of experiencing fear and anxiety feeds fear and anxiety, and it shrinks lives. Avoidance is toxic. It is *the* poison that turns normal anxiety and fear into a life-shattering problem. In fact, the weight of research clearly teaches us that avoidance of your emotional pain—although understandable—is simply bad for you and your life.

Toxic avoidance can take many forms, such as avoiding people, places, activities, and situations that might lead to anxious and fearful thoughts and feelings. Some people turn away by using and abusing alcohol and other drugs to numb out, forget, or dampen the impact of unpleasant and unwanted thoughts and feelings and situations that may trigger them. Others simply cut and run when they find themselves feeling anxiety, fear, and other forms of emotional pain.

Devoting yourself to not having anxiety and fear is quite limiting; it may come to define how you live your entire life. Avoidance gets in the way of the things you want to do and the directions you want to go. There's no way to approach a vital life while avoiding emotional and psychological pain. Nobody can move toward a full life while also moving away from the inevitable possibility of experiencing pain and difficulty along the way. So what can you do?

You do the opposite! Instead of running, struggling, and avoiding, you decide to stay with whatever is going on inside you. When old habits compel you to pull away, you learn to lean in. When you feel pulled to shut down and withdraw, you open up. You can think of this practice as a way of learning to stay with yourself.

This suggestion to do the opposite may surprise you. So it's important to be clear about why you're doing this. You do this not to wallow in the pain of anxiety and just stay there. You do this because staying with yourself and your anxiety is what allows you to move toward what you want to do in your life. So long as you turn away from the difficulty, the upset, the fear, you won't get to live your life. That's why you need to confront the avoidance—and change it. The next exercise will help you get started.

MAKING LIFE-AFFIRMING CHOICES

In this exercise, we'd like to help you identify more life-affirming alternatives to toxic acts of avoidance. On a piece of paper, mark two columns.

Label the left one "toxic avoidance" and the right one "doing the opposite."

- In the "toxic avoidance" column, list everything you do to avoid feeling anxious or afraid—every action, form of distraction, and coping strategy. Be specific; for example, "I stay in my cubicle to avoid seeing my boss because I'm afraid he will criticize my work."

- Now move to the right column and for each avoidance strategy, write down what would be the opposite; for example, "I won't go out of my way to avoid my boss; if I happen to see him in the hallway, I can simply say hello and keep walking."

The next time the toxic voice of avoidance speaks up, think *do the opposite*. When avoidance demands that you get smaller, think expansion, and then do something, even a baby step, that might be potentially life affirming. You'll notice that life-affirming alternatives to avoidance are often the exact opposite of what your mind was suggesting at first.

11 Taking a Leap

All choices and actions involve some risk. You simply don't know what the future holds and what you may find in life. Many people remain stuck because they're unwilling to risk taking a step, preferring the old and familiar, even if it's deadening. To get us out of this rut, life is asking each of us to choose to be willing—to risk stepping into the unknown—because that's how we grow.

In this sense, willingness is a leap of faith. It's like jumping off a diving board into a pool, not knowing exactly what the water temperature will be or what the experience will be like. This is quite different than wading into the pool, testing the waters, seeing if it is too hot, too cold, too dirty, and so on. Wading isn't willingness. It's gradual and conditional, and so you're left making choices based on how you feel or what you might think or feel.

Willingness as a leap means to show up and be open to experiencing everything that your mind and body may offer, not knowing exactly what you may find from one moment to the next. This stance is arms open wide; it's the opposite of fighting anxiety with all you've got. In fact, if you're willing, you can actually do it right now.

ARMS WIDE OPEN

Stand up for a moment (if you're sitting, that works too), open your arms as wide as you can, and keep them like that for a while. And while you're spreading your arms like this, allow all your experiences to come and be just what they are—make no attempt to change them. Open up to them all; really feel them and let them be.

Assuming this posture is great practice and can actually be fun. This willingness posture captures the essence of the LIVE approach you're practicing in this book. With arms open, you're receptive. Unrestricted, now you're allowing what's there anyway. This stance is needed to LIVE more fully, and without all the limitations imposed by the mind and feelings.

Here's why we think willingness is so powerful. Many people treat anxiety as their worst enemy. But what if anxiety isn't the enemy? What if you could learn to develop some kindness and compassion for all your experience—including anxiety—and for yourself? Struggling would no longer be necessary. You'd cut the fuel line to your anxieties, and new options would become available to you.

So when we encourage you to be willing, we're not asking you to like everything that life offers. As you step forward, willingness is asking you to open up to every aspect of your experience, fully, and without defense, because in opening you gain freedom to do what matters to you. You're practicing living fearlessly!

12 Voices of Anxiety

The human mind is a thought-generating machine. It's that voice inside your head, broadcasting twenty-four hours a day, seven days a week. That's what minds do. But not everything you think is helpful. You don't need to listen to each thought and do what it commands.

The voice of anxiety will offer an endless stream of thoughts covering all of your deep-seated fears and worries, and all that's wrong with you. On top of that, it tells you that you need to do something about it, or else! So it offers another stream of thoughts in the form of sensible-sounding solutions. "Breathe slowly. Take a pill. Watch TV. Go to bed early. Take it easy, call in sick." And so on. This voice comes from the well-established and familiar belief that anxiety and fear are somehow dangerous, that it's impossible to feel anxiety and still live a good life, that managing and controlling anxiety is the way out of misery and into happiness.

The voice is fooling you. It tells you that you need to control anxiety to be happy. Yet all that effort tends to make matters worse. To break free from this cycle, you'll need to learn to identify the voices of anxiety and all the unhelpful solutions they offer. The next exercise will help you learn to do just that.

DISCOVER UNHELPFUL THOUGHTS

Get yourself centered, and then reflect on the following questions. Listen for the voice of anxiety and what it commands you to do. Be specific and list each thought and each apparent solution. Write them down if you'd like.

- What does the voice of anxiety tell me that I need to do to about it when I'm right in the middle of feeling anxious or afraid?

- What does the voice of anxiety tell me I should not do so that I can prevent anxiety and fear from happening again?

Now think about each apparent solution, and reflect on these questions:

- Have any of them worked in the long term?

- Do any of these voices capture the essence of what you want to be about as a person?

- When you listen and do as the voices command, do you end up doing more or less with your life?

It takes practice to learn to catch the voices of anxiety and call them out for what they truly are. So, do that. Practice observing what anxiety commands you to do. Identify the voices of anxiety that limit you. When you learn to observe and label the voices as more thinking, you will create space to make wise, life-affirming choices. You don't have to blindly follow everything your anxious mind offers you.

This is also a great opportunity to again practice doing the opposite—the skill you learned in Chapter 10. Instead of listening to unhelpful voices in your head, you can choose to do the opposite of what they tell you to do. You may find that you end up doing more of what *you* really want to do rather than what your anxious mind commands you to do.

13 On Autopilot

"Mindless activity" is a popular catchphrase. It describes a common human experience that we know, and you know, all too well. Time and again, we've found ourselves going about our days, doing various tasks, with little or no awareness of what is going on around us.

If you've ever read the newspaper or a book and found your eyes at the bottom of the page without any idea how you got there, then you know what we mean.

The mind is a master conductor, orchestrating our bodies and experience. So much so, in fact, that we can literally lose contact with the world around us just as it is. We may then find ourselves living in our heads, in the world of thoughts, ideas, and images. This can leave us feeling disconnected from the world. Perhaps even disembodied. But you shouldn't fault yourself for that. The mind has a very difficult time staying wholly present with what's going on.

To get back in touch with your life and experience, you'll need to reprogram your mind. It needs to be taught to come back to the present and to what's going on as it is. There are many ways to retrain the mind, but here we'd like to suggest an activity you probably do all the time and mostly without conscious awareness of doing it: walking.

MINDFUL WALKING

Walking is a wonderful way to learn to be a skillful observer of your thoughts and feelings. The practice asks you to take conscious control over your experience. No longer at the mercy of the mind's endless edicts and wanderings, you learn that you—not your mind—are in charge of what you want to do and where you want to go.

Take yourself for a fifteen-minute walk. Focus on your breathing—deeply in and out—and walk naturally. Bring your awareness to the rhythm of your steps and how your body feels as it moves. If your mind wanders to other things, just notice that. Then gently bring your attention back to the experience of walking.

Notice the feel of your feet as they meet the ground with each step. Move your awareness to your hip area, your midsection, your arms and legs—experience how they move with each stride. See how your body is in perfect rhythm and flow.

Notice how you're moving with your thoughts and feelings too—all of them going forward. Sense the vitality in this movement. You control the steps you take and the directions you go.

Once you finish, take a few moments to reflect on your experience. What showed up for you as you walked? What was it like to walk with your mind? What was walking like as you became more consciously aware of the experience of walking?

As with any skill, learning to be a mindful observer takes practice. The good news is that life offers abundant opportunities to practice, and not just when you're walking. You can also practice being a mindful observer when mowing the lawn, taking a shower, brushing your teeth, driving in your car, doing the dishes, or having a conversation. As you bring mindful awareness into your life, you learn that you have the power to take your mind and emotional weather with you wherever you wish to go.

14 Whole, Complete, Enough

People struggling with anxiety are some of the strongest people we know. They're survivors. You probably are too!

But many are also very harsh with themselves. They believe that they're not good enough; that they're too weak; that they're not trying hard enough. Do you find yourself thinking this way too? You might think, "I'm somehow broken." Or worse, "I'm not good enough." It's in this place of lack, or "not enough," that struggle and shame find the spark that they need to grow.

This is the human mind at work, creating thoughts. Sometimes, thoughts will be harsh and judgmental. In fact, the mind can judge just about anything in the world around you and the world within you—beautiful, wonderful, likable, terrible, awful, and so on. It can even turn judgment on you—on the very essence of your being.

If you allow it, this darker side of the mind can invade more and more areas of your life, trapping you and keeping you stuck. But there's a healthy escape route, a way out of the clutches of this toxic thinking. It starts with catching the self-loathing before it consumes you.

In truth, you have everything you need. There's no such thing as a broken person. This is a judgment—a thought—

that the mind creates and applies to your experience over and over again. And it's a lifeless judgment at that.

You, and only you, can decide if you'll listen. You don't have to swallow everything your mind dishes out. This is an important and necessary first step to harness your capacity for self-kindness and compassion—one of the most powerful antidotes to suffering when your mind is unkind.

As you learn to do that, you'll discover that your life can be different. Your life need not be determined by what you think. You don't have to buy into unhelpful thoughts your mind feeds you. You can learn how to act on your anxiety differently!

WATCH THE JUDGMENT

Allow yourself to get settled and centered in a quiet space. Set the intention to make this your kind and gentle space. Take a moment or two and consider what your mind tells you about you and your anxiety problem. How does your mind beat you up and beat you down? Look for the "I'm not enough" message. Inside that message is the idea that it's not okay to be you. If you allow this to take over your life, you'll naturally struggle to change what you think and what you feel, because your mind is telling you "It's not okay; you're not okay just as you are." And before you know it, your mind has drawn you back into another round of tug-of-war!

- Become aware of the labels your mind creates about you, your feelings, your self-worth as a person, and your life.

- Pick one judgment or label and imagine projecting those words onto a giant movie screen in front of you.

- See the words, the letters, the color of the ink, and the limitations and lifelessness in those thoughts. Notice that you can observe the judgment. Notice that the words are not you. You can simply look at them without blindly believing them.

- As you look, don't get into an argument with your mind about the truth of the thoughts. Truth is far less important compared with helpful. The only thing that really matters now is whether a particular thought is helping you move forward or keeping you stuck where you are.

- Breathe gently into each projection, each judgment, with a sense of peace and kind allowing.

- Allow the projections to come and go, and sink into an inner knowing that you are so much more than the projections that your mind manufactures about you.

See if you can bring this observing awareness into the experiences of each day whenever old, lifeless, and limiting thoughts pop into your awareness and try to keep you stuck. Connect with the inner voice inside you, calling out that you are whole, complete, and enough as you are!

15 Kindness and Self-Care

Many people can be very hard on themselves. You may be hard on yourself, too. You might ask yourself, "Why can't I snap out of it? This is so stupid. I know it's all in my head. I'm angry at myself, and I'm angry at the world. I hate my panic attacks—I just hate them."

All this blaming and hating isn't the solution. In fact, it creates the conditions for things to get worse. There's no sugarcoating this point. When you meet negative emotional energy with more negative energy in the form of self-judgment and blame, you will suffer more.

What you need is a shift in perspective. This shift asks you to decide, perhaps for the first time, to change your relationship with your mind, body, and experience. Instead of blaming and hating, you can decide to take care of your own house—your mind, body, emotional life, and anything else that your old history throws at you.

There are only two ways to go here. You can create a house that is hostile and unkind or one full of friendliness and kindness. Acting with kindness toward yourself means acting in a caring and loving way. Here, you practice treating yourself—mind, body, and spirit—as you would treat someone or something you love and cherish. This is a choice only you can make.

Practicing acts of kindness toward yourself is a potent remedy for anxiety, anger, regret, shame, and depression. This practice will make it easier for you to stop fighting with your mind and body. It's a simple thing you can do to bring more peace and joy to your life.

PRACTICE BEING GOOD TO YOURSELF

Start each day by setting an intention, before you get out of bed in the morning, to practice at least one act of kindness toward yourself. Be unwavering in your commitment to follow through during the day.

Think about something you could do to be kind to yourself. Be specific and write it down. This could involve taking time to practice meditation, reading a good book, going for a walk, listening to music, gardening, or preparing a good meal. Or it might take the form of treating yourself in a kind and loving way when life is unkind, or when your mind and body offer you experiences that are unpleasant. Here, think how you might respond if someone else you care for was in your shoes, going through what you're going through.

How would you treat this person? Then apply that same tone of voice and kind heart to your experience.

Be mindful that you do this not because you have accomplished something special to deserve it. And this isn't about being selfish. You do it because it matters to your health and well-being. Call it an act of self-care if that helps. You are worthy of kindness because you have a heart and are alive. We all are worthy of kindness, and not just on special occasions. Self-kindness and love are available to us all the time and any time.

So whenever you need kindness, you don't have to wait until other people are kind to you. You can choose to respond to your needs any time by showing tender loving care toward yourself. When you do, you're building the inner strength you need to create your best life!

16 Cultivating Allowing

We've met countless people who have struggled with anxiety. And, at some point, many of them have said "I know—I just need to accept my anxiety." They think acceptance means giving up. Eventually, they stop making any effort to change. But this isn't what acceptance asks of us.

Acceptance is really a choice to open up and be with whatever is happening anyway, just as it is. But you cannot accept what you do not know. And you cannot accept what you resist and are hostile toward.

So, to accept something means to make space for it and to allow it to be there. You also need to be willing to look at what makes you feel uneasy. This is where learning to be more mindful and present can make a huge difference.

Mindfulness exercises teach us that we cannot choose what comes into our minds and what we feel. We can choose only what we pay attention to, how we pay attention, and what we do. This will help you to see your difficult experiences more clearly and to show up more fully to the sweet moments in your life too.

But without kindness and compassion, there's no healthy way to allow anxiety or any other unpleasant emotional experiences to be there. Instead, it will feel like you're holding a ticking time bomb just waiting for it to explode and doing nothing about it. But you can hold your pain gently, and with some curiosity and compassion. This can transform and defuse the pain into something you can carry, honor, and perhaps even learn from and grow through. This is why we want you to remember to cultivate acceptance in your life.

The following exercise will help you do just that. It will teach you how to stay with your anxieties with loving-kindness toward yourself, bringing as much warmth and compassion into the situation as you can. This is a concrete way of learning that anxiety isn't your enemy.

ALLOWING THOUGHTS AND FEELINGS

- Get into a comfortable seated position and allow your eyes to close gently.

- Take a few moments to get in touch with the movement of your breath and the sensations in your body. As you do that, slowly bring your attention to the gentle rising and falling of your breath in your chest and belly.

- Breathe naturally and, as best you can, bring an attitude of generous allowing and gentle acceptance to your experience, just as it is.

- Sooner or later your mind will wander away from the breath to other concerns, thoughts, worries, images, bodily sensations, planning, or daydreams, or it may just drift along. When you notice your mind wandering, just acknowledge that and gently, and with kindness, come back to your breath.

- If you become aware of feelings, tension, or other intense physical sensations, just notice them, acknowledge their presence, and see if you can make space for them. Imagine with each inhalation you are creating more space within you.

- You may notice sensations in your body and how they change from moment to moment. Breathe calmly into and out from the sensations in any region of the body where you feel discomfort, imagining the breath moving into and out from those places.

- Along with physical sensations in your body, you may also notice thoughts about the sensations—and thoughts about the thoughts. If that happens, just notice them and return to the breath and the present moment, as it is. Thoughts are thoughts, physical sensations are physical sensations, feelings are feelings, nothing more, nothing less.

• Notice how thoughts and feelings come and go in your mind and body. Yet your breath is always with you in each moment. And that wise observer part of you is always with you too. This observer part of you can notice all the experiences you may have. You are the place and space for your experiences. You are not what your thoughts and feelings say, no matter how persistent or intense they may be. Make that space a kind space, a gentle space, a loving space, a welcome home.

• Then, when you're ready, gradually widen your attention to take in the sounds around you, and slowly open your eyes with the intention to bring mindful acceptance into the remaining moments of your day.

This exercise can be challenging to do at first. But don't let that judgment stand in the way of repeating it over the weeks to come. Remember that acceptance is a skill that grows with practice. The goal is to develop the skill so that you can then apply it in your life, anytime and anyplace.

There's no right or wrong way to practice. So be kind with yourself as you do the practice. The important thing is that you commit to doing this exercise on the path to becoming a better observer and full participant in your life.

17 Popping the Illusion

There is something magical about watching a very young child at play. Children are often utterly present in the moment, unencumbered by an endless stream of thoughts. But as they grow, very quickly that sense of presence recedes as they develop ways to think and communicate about themselves and their world using language and other forms of symbolic communication.

As adults we often fail to see that words are powerful ways to share experiences, but they're nothing like the real thing. Thinking about sitting in a comfy chair is nothing like the experience of actually sitting in a comfy chair.

But as we swim in language and thought, we often end up taking thoughts literally, treating them as if they were the same as the experiences they describe. If our thoughts are left unchecked, we lose sight of the fact that the mind produces thoughts in the form of images and words. Instead, we see them as real physical things that can threaten our very being.

But if you can step back a little, you'll begin to notice that thoughts are just a bunch of words, with no real form or substance. This will open your mind to more than the automatic conclusions and reactions you may draw from those words. The next exercise will help you see for yourself that thoughts are just words too.

PLAYING WITH THOUGHTS

Let's start with the word "spider." When you think "spider," what does it look like in your mind? Can you see it crawling? If spiders scare you in real life, you may even feel a little anxious or disgusted. Now sit where you can see a clock. Say that word "spider" out loud, over and over, as fast as you can: "Spider, spider, spider…" Do it for exactly forty seconds.

When you're done, reflect on what happened to the meaning of the word after forty seconds. Did it still make you feel creepy (if you felt creepy)? And did it continue to summon the image of the spider? Or, did the words start running together, morphing into an odd sound—"ider, ider, ider…"? Notice too how quickly the meaning of the word dissolves during those forty seconds.

Right now, repeat the exercise. But this time use a thought you tell yourself when you're anxious or afraid—something that gets you tangled up and struggling. Give it a one-word name, like "worry," "panic," "anxious," "alone," "sadness," "death," "dirtiness," "sickness," "heights," or "crowds." You may use a judgmental word, like "ugly," "stupid," "worthless," or "boring." It might even hurt or make you mad to think this word.

Now say that word out loud as fast as you can for about forty seconds. Then stop and reflect. Does the word still sound as believable as it once did? Can you see how it's also just a word, a sound without form or substance?

This powerful exercise teaches us that the mind can create an illusion of anxiety monsters that are really not monsters at all. The monsters are words, linked with images and sounds, that have meanings that you've learned to give them. When you understand that about the mind, you'll develop your capacity to get unhooked from its many snares. You'll also learn to see that *you* are not what you *think*.

18 Not Buying It

Like a skilled salesperson, the mind is constantly offering us thoughts and hoping that we buy whatever it offers. Sometimes the mind offers useful and life-affirming thoughts. These are certainly worthy of our attention. But often the products of the human mind are not helpful. When you buy into unhelpful thoughts, you'll know it, because it leaves you feeling more anxious and with a deep sense that your life is getting smaller.

You can learn to break this cycle. To do that, you'll need to recognize your thoughts and images for what they really are. Thoughts! But, as the next exercise teaches us, there's an important distinction between you and the products of your mind. This simple and powerful exercise will help you when your mind is trying to get you to buy into unhelpful thoughts.

HAVING SECOND THOUGHTS?

The practice here is simple, but it will take some getting used to. Whenever you have a thought, preface it with "I'm having the thought that…" For example, when you say or think "I'll have a panic attack if I go out," you can think or say out loud, "I'm having the thought that I'll have a panic attack if I go out." Or if you find yourself thinking, "I need to get a handle on my anxiety or my life will go downhill," you can say out loud, "I'm having the thought that I need to get a handle on my anxiety or my life will go downhill." The practice is to notice that you're having thoughts.

You can apply the same strategy to scary images or feelings. With images you can say to yourself, "I'm having the image that [insert an image that bothers you]." With feelings, you can say to yourself, "I'm having the feeling that I'm about to die" or "I'm having the feeling that [insert what you typically feel]."

If you find this too clumsy or difficult, there's an even simpler way of labeling. Whenever any thought comes up, just label it thinking: "There's thinking." Whenever an image comes up, tell yourself "There's a picture." And when physical sensations come up, just label each of them, one at a time, as "There's a sensation."

Practice doing this deliberately with anything your mind or body offers you. This will give you space to see your thoughts and emotional experiences for what they are—products of your mind that need not always be listened to, trusted, or believed.

It takes a while to develop these new labeling and language habits. It'll probably feel awkward at first. Just stay the course and keep practicing. These new skills will help you see thoughts as thoughts, images as images, and feelings as feelings. Even when the most intense and scary thoughts, images, or feelings seem highly believable, remind yourself that they're still only thoughts, images, or feelings. This will give you the space you need to move forward when your anxieties and fears show up. You don't need to buy into everything your mind dishes out.

19 Getting Unstuck

It can be very hard to move forward when your mind tells you to stay right where you are because it's safer, less risky. When you're anxious or afraid, your mind may even conjure up all kinds of reasons why you should either just stay put or run. But it's important to understand that your mind is baiting a trap that ultimately keeps you stuck, far from the life you wish to have.

The most dangerous of those traps comes in the form of reasons and a litany of justifications for running away from anxiety instead of staying with it. Your mind may say, "You'll make a fool of yourself if you go to the show, or do this or that." It may proclaim, "If you panic, then you might hurt yourself (or someone else), embarrass yourself, or even die. It may declare, "You can't go to the show because you'll fall apart, have a nervous breakdown, be unable to cope or breathe, or lose all control." All of these thoughts bait you to just sit on your hands and do nothing.

More deeply, your mind is saying, "You can't have anxiety and live your life!" But you certainly can live your life with or without anxiety. This takes some courage on your part. Courage is the decision that something else is more important than the fear.

When your anxious mind tries to trap you, sitting still with your thoughts and not doing what they say is one of the most courageous things you can do. It's courageous because the impulse to cut and run, or avoid, is so strong and automatic. Doing nothing about anxious thoughts and feelings is the more difficult path.

Your mind will be screaming at you to listen to it, just as you've always done. But you don't need to listen, even when your mind is throwing a tantrum. You can simply watch your thoughts as thoughts. And if you stay committed to this practice, you'll find that it'll get easier to observe and just take note of thoughts, images, and urges rather than doing as they say.

One simple way to get started is with mind watching. When you practice watching your mind, you learn to be an observer instead of taking in and swallowing whatever nasty-looking stuff your mind dishes out. You learn how to spot when your mind is baiting you with thoughts that not only keep you stuck, but also make you anxious and afraid, and may even leave you feeling bad about yourself. This next exercise will get you started.

MIND WATCHING

- Get in a comfortable place where you won't be disturbed for five to ten minutes. Begin by closing your eyes and taking a series of slow, deep breaths.

- Imagine your mind is a medium-sized white room with two doors. Thoughts come in through the front door and leave through the back door.

- Simply watch each thought as it enters the white room. Don't analyze it. Don't engage or argue with it. Don't believe or disbelieve it. Just acknowledge having the thought—that's all. Acknowledge it and do nothing with it. Keep on watching the thought until it leaves. When the thought seems like it wants to go, then let it go. Don't try to hold on to it.

- Keep breathing, keep watching. A thought doesn't require you to react; it doesn't make you do anything; it doesn't mean you're less of a person for having it.

- Again, watch and notice your thoughts and treat them as if they were visitors passing in and out of the white room. Let them have their brief moment on the stage. Then, when they're ready to go, let them leave, and greet and label the next thought—and the next.

- Continue this exercise until you sense a real emotional distance from your thoughts. Wait until even the judgments are just a moment in the room—no longer important, no longer requiring action.

- Practice this exercise at least once a day.

The key to this *Mind Watching* exercise is to notice and observe judgmental and other unwanted thoughts rather than getting caught up in them. The more you practice being an observer, the more you'll be able to let any thought come and go without it controlling you. Make an intention to do that. Recognizing how mind traps keep you stuck is an important skill. It's also a critical step out of the struggle-and-avoidance trap. This is how you'll get your freedom back.

20 Humanizing the Mind

You've met people you don't like very much—we all have. These people may annoy you. They may even scare you, revealing your deepest fears and vulnerabilities. Their words and actions are unwelcome, perhaps upsetting, and yet they prod you in ways that hurt. And you end up feeling bad.

Your mind can be like one of these people—bullying and taunting you. Here you can benefit from getting some perspective. One simple way is to ask yourself, "Who's telling me that right now?" If your anxious mind were a person standing behind you, would you really want to listen to that person? Has this person given you useful advice in the past?

But this may seem a bit too abstract. So let's do another exercise, created by John's wife Jamie, to make this teaching more concrete. You may wish to jot down your answers on a piece of paper.

WHO AM I DEALING WITH?

Begin by getting in touch with your anxious or fearful mind. Focus on the unsettling messages your mind feeds you about you and your life before, during, or after you're anxious or afraid.

Now let's see what this mind of yours would be like if it were a person you'd just met. Go ahead and imagine this for a moment. Close your eyes, if that helps you create a clearer image.

Imagine what this person is like in as much detail as you possibly can. What kind of personality does your anxious mind have? What kind of person are you dealing with here? Is this a caring, loving person, or someone who is critical, harsh, and opinionated? Is this someone you'd like to spend time with? Would you want to be friends or have this person over for dinner?

Now let's fill in some details. Is this person male or female? How old is he or she? What does the person's face look like? What does the person's body look like? How tall is the person, and what does he or she normally wear? How does this person carry himself or herself?

Now go further. How does this person sound? Loud? Opinionated? Boastful? Negative? Nagging? Does the person speak with an accent?

Then step back for a moment and ask yourself: Who is this person? Give the person a name—don't be afraid to choose a funny one. Take time to reflect.

Once you have this character clearly in your mind, imagine that she or he shows up on your doorstep one day uninvited. As you open the door slowly, ask yourself: What is my reaction to seeing this character? Am I choosing to greet this person in a loving way, perhaps as a dear friend or family member? Or do I choose to greet the anxiety character as an enemy or unwelcome guest? You might be ambivalent. Notice here that treating anxiety with ambivalence or as an enemy would not be something you would hope for in a healthy relationship with another person in your life. This is where things need to change.

If your anxious mind were a real person like the character you just created, would you really want to listen to everything the person had to say? Would you let the person dictate what you do and when? Probably not. So choose the kind of relationship you wish to have with your mind and emotional life.

21 Words, Letters, and Ink

Thoughts can seem solid, with form and substance, like giant rocks weighing you down. But this is a great illusion. In truth, thoughts are like smoke wafting up from a burning incense stick. We may try to grab the smoke, but it eludes us. We may try to hold on to the smoke, but it slips through our fingers. Eventually, the smoke dissipates and there's nothing left. No lasting trace. Nothing to grasp at. This is the true nature of thoughts—words and images without form and substance.

Learning to see the real nature of thoughts is a powerful way to pop the illusion that you are your thoughts, or that all thoughts must be listened to and believed.

The next exercise will help you further cultivate this important skill.

THOUGHTS ON CARDS

This exercise can be done anytime and anywhere that anxious thoughts and urges show up. All you need are some small pieces of paper or index cards. When your anxieties and fears show up, simply label them, placing each thought, worry, sensation, urge, or image on its own card. Be specific!

Next, look at what you put down on the card. If we asked you to describe what you see, what would you tell us? Your first reaction may be, "I see the words...duh." But here we want you to get more granular. What do you actually see on the card? Just focus on what you wrote down.

If you take a moment and just focus on what your eyes see, you'll notice that you see words, letters, and ink. That's it. If you wrote down "I am incompetent" and look at that, you'll see words, letters, and ink. If what you wrote was "I am a banana," you'll see the same thing: words, letters, and ink. All thoughts are made up of the same stuff.

A moment ago, the thoughts and urges were inside your head. They probably seemed really hard and heavy in there. Now they're out, exposed, and you can look at them. Allow yourself time to see them for what they are. What happens when you turn your life over to the words, letters, and ink on the card? Notice that you have a choice to do what the card says—to struggle—or you can allow what you wrote to be just as it is: a thought, a sensation, an image, an urge to act. Just words, letters, and ink.

To get a sense of the struggle, place the card with the thought or urge on it between your hands and push your hands together really hard. Do this for at least thirty seconds and then stop. Gently place the card on your lap. Notice the difference in effort between pushing against the thought or urge compared to the experience of the card gently resting on your lap.

It's very helpful to practice holding your thoughts and urges by carrying them with you. To do that, place the cards in your pocket, purse, or briefcase as you go about your daily activities. Notice that you can move with them.

Once in a while, when you have a moment during the day, take the cards out and look at them, but make sure you don't get hooked by what they say—just look and observe. Remind yourself what you're really looking at—words, letters, and ink. Notice that you have a choice: to get caught up in the thoughts you see on the cards, or to do something else in your life. If you look to your experience for advice, you'll know what to do. It's time to trust your experience, not what your anxious mind says.

Practice putting your thoughts and urges on cards and taking them with you wherever you go. Do this every day for as long as you wish. If you like, you can change the cards from time to time. Some people we've worked with tell us that they prepare a stack of index cards. Then, every morning, they shuffle them and pick four or five different cards and carry them around for the day. The cards will be there any time you wish to attend to them, just as your old history is always with you.

Remember, every time you happen to touch or read a card during the day without getting tangled up in what it says, or doing as it says, you're honing an important skill. Over time, you'll notice a sense of detachment from the pull that those words have had on you for so long.

22 Be Patient

Learning to watch thoughts come and go in the white room and move with them as you did with mindful walking are great skills that you can use daily. But when anxiety and fear show up and become more intense, they can drain away your hope and abiding intention to stay with yourself. It can seem nearly impossible to be inside your own skin and stay where you are. We naturally want to get away from discomfort. The urge to do something can be painfully strong, with the energy and explosive force of an intense storm. This can leave you feeling out of control and frightened.

You can learn to ride along with the energy inside—the thunder of your impulses, the lightning of your fear, the relentless uncertainty of your anxiety, or the pounding wind and rain that drives your tendency to cut and run. This takes some courage. You can practice just being with it, without letting it blow you away. This is another powerful way to live fearlessly—a life that is not dictated by fear.

THIS TOO SHALL PASS

- Get comfortable in your chair and allow your eyes to close gently. Take a few moments to notice the natural rhythm of your breath as you breathe in and out.

- As you settle, bring to mind a recent situation where you felt the strong urge to cut and run from your fear and anxiety. Bring the situation alive in your mind as best you can. Where were you? Who else was there? What happened? What did you experience then, and what are you experiencing again right now?

- As you bring the situation to mind, notice the storm of anxiety or fear rolling in. Notice any turbulent physical changes in your body, including pain, pressure, or other scary sensations. There may be lightning strikes of thoughts, perhaps about your sensations and feelings. What's your mind telling you about them? About the situation? About you?

- Next, bring your attention to the physical experience of the urge to act. Notice the wild energy there, as the pounding rain tries to wash away your resolve and all that you care about. Is there pressure, tightness, or tension? If so, where is it located? Does it have a shape? A color?

- Now, choose to ride out the storm. Imagine
  opening up, arms wide open, and staying with
  the wild energy below the surface of your
  experience. If you can, go ahead and open
  your arms as wide as you can. Open up to
  your experience without trying to fix it, fight
  it, or suppress it, and without acting on it.
  Just stay there, your arms still wide open,
  bringing understanding and kindness to the
  energy and discomfort, as you would do for a
  dear friend or loved one who is in pain and
  needs your help.

- Notice as the storm front within you eventually starts to move on. Notice as things begin
  to quiet down and become still. And, as you
  rest in that stillness, notice what's new or different for you. See if you can connect with
  having done something good for yourself, for
  your life—even if you were scared, feeling the
  strong urge to run or lash out.

- As this time for practice comes to an end,
  acknowledge and honor the step you took
  with this exercise, and commit to practicing
  riding out your difficult urges in the service
  of living the life you want.

This exercise teaches you that anxiety and fear come and go of their own accord. Often, there's no healthy way to control your emotional weather. But you can always choose how you respond to it. Each storm is an opportunity to practice being open, mindful, and present with yourself just as you are. This will help you stay with yourself when anxiety and fear threaten to block your path. You can do it anytime you find yourself feeling unpleasant emotions.

23 Disarming Anxiety

Anxiety and fear draw power and energy from your active participation. When you feel stuck in fear or anxiety, it's likely that the monster is serving up barriers in the form of thoughts, bodily sensations, images, or urges that you'd rather not experience. So you struggle. You avoid. You resist. You may even give up. But this way of relating with your emotional life is exactly what the anxiety needs from you to grow into a menacing monster.

In the next exercise, you'll learn how to disarm the anxiety monster so that it's no longer a barrier between you and the life you wish to lead. The practice is learning to be present, to open up, and to nurture qualities of kindness with yourself and your experience. This is not about killing the anxiety monster, because we know that's impossible. It's not about shutting your mind off from dishing out odd, scary, disturbing images and judgmental thoughts. The key is to acknowledge all of this without feeding it with your active resistance.

As with the other exercises, there's no right or wrong way to do this exercise. Just follow along as best you can.

TAKING IT APART,
PIECE BY PIECE

- Get in a comfortable position in your chair. Allow your eyes to close gently. Take a couple of gentle breaths in…and out…in…and out.

- Now see if for just a moment you can be present with the anxiety monster. Notice how the monster is made up of a number of pieces—thoughts, images, physical sensations in your body, and urges to fight and resist. Now let's take it apart, piece by piece.

- One by one, focus on each part, and see if you can allow that part of the monster, and other aspects of your experience, to just be. Open your heart to each one of them and as much as you can, welcome them as part of your experience. Is any piece of the anxiety monster really your enemy?

- And as we get ready to close this exercise, gently ask yourself this: Am I willing to be gentle with my thoughts and feelings, and whatever my mind and body does, and accept them as part of myself? And are my life and my values important enough to me to be

willing to do this now, and perhaps again and
again?

- Then, when you're ready, gradually widen
  your attention to take in the sounds around
  you, then slowly open your eyes, with the
  intention to bring this awareness of just being
  as you are to the present moment and the rest
  of the day.

This exercise teaches us that anxiety is made up of
many smaller parts. Looking at the parts, one by one, is a
powerful way to deflate anxiety. Many of the parts that
make up anxiety are familiar to you and not really worth
fighting against. That so-called monster is made up of
thoughts (images, memories, words), physical sensations,
and behavioral urges and reactions. Are the ingredients in
this mix really your enemy? Perhaps anxiety is really no
monster at all.

24 Who Am I, *Really?*

Most people are bewildered if you ask them, "Who are you?" They might say, "My name is..." while pointing at their body. Often they may answer in terms of their roles in life, such as mother, coach, construction worker, lawyer, receptionist, artist. But is this who we really are? Our body? Our roles? Are you the same person now as you were when you were six years old? Do you call yourself a first grader?

If you persistently ask yourself "Who am I?" your mind will come up with self-descriptions such as "I am an anxious woman," "I am a kind person," "I am not good at math," and so on. Sometimes the answers are not just one-line statements but include long stories about why you've become the person you are today.

There's nothing wrong with telling stories, as long as you keep in mind that they're still only stories. As plausible as they might seem, they're still stories—words about you, your past, and your possible future—being created by your mind all the time. The stories may contain some dark events that you've lived through. We're not telling you your past is unimportant. Rather, we're encouraging you to take an honest look at the stories that your mind creates and ask, "Are these stories really helpful to me, right now?"

If you really believe these stories and do as they say, they can turn from mind traps into utterly self-defeating life traps—keeping you literally stuck right where you are. So if you tell yourself in the morning that you've always been an anxious person, along with ten reasons why you've become such a person, and then end up staying at home because you felt anxious after waking up, now is the time to pause and take stock. Are these stories life expanding or life constricting? Are they helpful in moving you toward the life you wish to lead?

At this point, you may wonder, "Well, if I'm not my body, or what I think, feel, do, or what others say about me, then who the heck am I?"

WHO AM I?

Take a look at the following list of statements. Notice what happens inside of you when you read the first four statements. Then move on to complete the last four statements with troubling descriptions that your mind offers up to you regularly.

- I am an anxious person.

- I am too shy.

- I am not good enough.

- I am never going to make it.

- I am _____.

- I am _____.

- I am not _____.

- I am not _____.

Did you notice how your mind almost immediately started working on these statements, perhaps agreeing or disagreeing with them, rephrasing or qualifying them, making them stronger, toning them down, and so on? Your mind has learned to respond to "I am" with a thought or an elaborate narrative. The mind's job is to come up with an answer when you ask it a question like "Who am I?" or "Why can't I do what I'd like to do?" This is important to understand. Your mind's answers are not you. They are simply more thinking, more thoughts.

Answering the question "Who am I, really?" with a simple, disarming "*I am*" allows you to drop all those unhelpful answers your mind constantly dishes out to you. It's the simplest and easiest way to let go of self-limiting thoughts—once and for all, any time. No more arguments, explanations, justifications, or the like. "*I am!*" In Chapter 27 we will introduce you to a simple, powerful meditation technique what will help you make experiencing "*I am*" a daily reality.

25 The Expansive Self

There's an important distinction between you and the stuff you've been struggling with. You are the one who can notice and observe the stuff going on in your mind, body, and world. But the stuff you think, feel, and experience is not you. You *have* thoughts, feelings, and experiences, but they *are not* you. Likewise, anxiety *is not* you! You may *have* anxiety, but it *is not* you!

There would be no way to observe a thought or feeling if you were it. But you can observe your thoughts, feelings, and physical sensations just as you do objects and experiences in the world around you. Like clouds in the sky, thoughts and feelings come and go by themselves. You can't make them go away. You can't hold on to them either. But you can learn to observe them without becoming them.

Although we sense experiences around us all the time, *we* are not those things we see, taste, smell, touch, and hear. We are just observing them. But we're not used to looking at our thoughts and emotional life from this perspective. And so we get trapped into thinking that we really are what we think and feel. This is a great setup for suffering.

To help us get a feel for the observer self, our Australian colleague Russ Harris came up with a simple weather metaphor.

THE SPACIOUS BLUE SKY

Your observer self is like the sky. Your thoughts and feelings are like the weather. The weather changes all the time, but no matter how bad it gets, the weather cannot harm the sky. Not even the worst thunderstorm, wildest cyclone, or coldest snowstorm can hurt the sky. And no matter how bad the weather may get, the sky has sufficient space for it all. And if we're willing to stick around, sooner or later we'll witness the weather getting better. Sometimes we forget that the sky is there, because we can't see it through all those dark clouds. But if we go high enough, even the darkest, heaviest rain clouds cannot prevent us from eventually reaching the clear sky. That open sky space extends in all directions, without borders, and is without beginning or end.

Your true self is the sky, not the weather. Like the sky, it is expansive. Meditation is probably the most effective and easiest way to contact this sense of self as an open, safe space right inside of you. But you can also develop the skill by consciously choosing to shift your perspective.

When you find yourself hardening or getting caught up in difficult thoughts and feelings, consciously become aware that you are the sky, step back from the difficulty as you might step back to look at a car you're thinking about buying, and look at the thoughts and feelings from the safe refuge of your observer self. From there you can watch what's going on and make space for even the most difficult thoughts and feelings—so ultimately they can no longer touch or hurt you. Thus you can gain great strength and freedom from cultivating the observer perspective.

26 Let It Be

A great source of suffering is getting attached to wanting more of something and less of something else. This condition is easy to spot when you feel anxious or afraid: you want less anxiety and more peace and joy. If you're bored, you want more excitement. If you're unhappy, you want more happiness.

"Want" literally means a lack or deficiency. So when you want your thoughts and feelings to be different, your mind is essentially telling you that *you* are lacking or deficient. Not only does that hurt, but it's also a great setup for struggle.

This is when nurturing your observer self can be very useful. As an observer, you watch what's going on and learn to allow your experience to be just as it is without *wanting* it to be different.

Let's see what a fictitious game of chess can teach us about looking at your experience from an impartial observer perspective, without wanting to pick sides, or doing so.

TO PLAY OR WATCH THE GAME?

Imagine you're part of a chess game. The dark pieces represent your anxieties and fears and everything that might trigger them. The light pieces represent your typical counterstrikes, each and every coping strategy you use to deal with anxiety and fear.

So when the dark knight attacks (for example, "I'm about to lose it"), you get on the back of the white knight, ride into battle armed with your coping strategies, and try to use them to knock the dark knight out: breathe…distract…think positive thoughts…procrastinate…leave the situation…give up…and on and on.

But this is not your typical chess game. In this game, we don't have two different players, each taking sides. Instead, the two opposing teams are really one team: you! The thoughts, feelings, and actions on both sides of the board are your thoughts, feelings, and actions. They all belong to you.

In this way, the game is rigged. Both sides will always know the other's moves. Worse, no matter which side wins now and then, one part of you will always be a loser. There's really no way to come out a winner when your own thoughts and feelings compete against each other.

Let's step back for a moment. What if those chess pieces aren't you, anyway? Can you imagine what a great relief it would be if you didn't need to be a player with a stake in the outcome? Can you see who else you might be?

Let's suppose you're the board. As the board, your job is to hold all the pieces. The board doesn't care about winners or losers. The board does not take sides or get involved in the battle. It just provides space for the game and allows it to happen.

As the board, you can choose to be an impartial observer of your experiences.

Thinking of yourself as a chessboard may seem odd, at least at first. But over time, taking the perspective of the board will become easier and it will provide tremendous relief. This relief is based on a deeper experience and understanding of who you really are.

As the board, you'll see that your thoughts and feelings are always coming and going, morphing and changing from one moment to the next. They're a part of you only for a while, and then they leave. But the board—that observer you—is and always has been there, unchanged by anything that goes on around it. It provides space to choose what to engage in, what to let go, and what to do with your time and energy. Learning to take the perspective of the board will give you both freedom from fear and greater peace of mind!

27 Drop the Stories

The mind is a highly evolved storytelling machine. Some of it may be useful, entertaining even. But the stories can also be confining, adding to your sense of stuckness and suffering.

One way to move past self-limiting thoughts and stories is to first let go of the idea that you are what you think and feel. This is where the observer self and mindfulness and self-compassion can help. You must also be willing to drop the rest of the story and labels that follow "*I am*," as you did in Chapter 24.

So, instead of "I am anxious," you notice that you are having a thought, and you ask yourself if that thought is really helpful as far as your life is concerned. If the answer is no, then you pause and bring your awareness back to that observer you, or "*I am*." Period. What follows "*I am*" are words—your mind at work creating the rest of the story.

But to really contact your essence, your true abiding sense of self, you'll need to dive below the words and the stories. Just below the surface, you'll find your observer self—the self that was and is always with you. It was there before you even had words to describe yourself. It was there yesterday and will be there tomorrow. It's your steadfast safe refuge.

There is this space right inside of you—a stillness that is deep within you and is waiting for you to contact it. Thousands of years of wisdom—and now, scientific research—support meditation practice as a powerful way to experience this safe, whole, and pristine aspect of you. Here, we'd like to introduce you to a very old form of meditation that will bring you into contact with your observer self and help you drop the story lines that often follow your unhelpful "I am this or that" narratives.

The next exercise, the *I Am Mantra Meditation*, asks you to repeat a simple phrase or mantra—"*I am.*" This practice quite literally makes you drop the story lines that typically used to follow your unhelpful "I am this or that" descriptions. As you silently repeat the "*I am*" mantra, your mind will settle deeply inward—in a natural, effortless way—below its bubbling surface to a place of pure consciousness and stillness. It will move you beyond your mind's endless chatter and give you the experience of silence and pure awareness—your true self.

At first, you'll get only brief glimpses of this experience, but over time simply closing your eyes and gently thinking the mantra will settle your mind. With regular practice this simple meditation will become a very powerful and transformational habit.

Read the instructions carefully, at least twice, before you start. As you do, pay attention to the few basic rules and directions. Then close your eyes and begin the meditation.

In the beginning, do the meditation for at least ten minutes. If you like, you can slowly extend your meditation time up to twenty minutes.

I AM MANTRA MEDITATION

- Get in a comfortable position in your chair. Sit upright with your hands resting in your lap. Your legs can either be uncrossed or crossed. Allow your eyes to close gently.

- Simply let your breath flow naturally without attempting to influence it.

- Wait for twenty to thirty seconds, then start thinking the mantra *"I am"* very gently and without any effort or strain. Repeat the mantra silently to yourself without worrying about its tempo, rhythm, or sound.

- After a while you'll notice thoughts or images or perhaps some bodily sensations. If a thought, image, or sensation comes, don't try to push it out. Instead, just allow it to be there. When you become aware that you're not thinking the mantra, quietly and gently come back to thinking the mantra, softly, faintly: *"I am... I am..."* So whenever you return to the mantra, do so ever so gently, in a faint and subtle way.

- The mantra may change in different ways. That's okay. It can get faster or slower, louder or softer, clearer or fainter, or it may not appear to change at all. Don't try to make a rhythm of the mantra or align it with your breathing. In every case, just take it as it comes, neither anticipating nor resisting change, approaching the whole exercise with ease.

- Continue this process for the next ten to twenty minutes.

- Then stop thinking the mantra and take a little time to rest in the stillness and silence of your meditation. Continue to sit with eyes closed for the next two to three minutes. Then open your eyes and resume your regular activities.

We suggest that you practice the *I Am Mantra Meditation* twice a day. Committing to a regular practice of daily meditation is one of the most important and powerful steps you can take toward healing and transformation. We know this from our own personal experience, and there is also much scientific research supporting this conclusion. This meditation will help you create space between your true self and your thoughts and emotions that have kept you stuck and struggling. In the beginning, be sure to reread the brief instructions first before you start your meditation.

28 Behavior Matters!

Behavior is anything you can do with your mouth, hands, and feet. When anxiety and fear show up, you likely respond with behavior to reduce them, make them go away, or get away from them. You may not realize that *you* have the power to control your behavior and how you respond to anxiety and fear. Learning to act differently is the key to getting unstuck.

Let's say you're in the mall and feel a panic attack coming on. Then you act on it. Perhaps you take one of the pills you carry with you at all times and then head for the exit. These are both behaviors.

But you could do something else. Instead of leaving, you could stay in the mall, use the skills in this book, and focus on doing what really matters to you. If you're really shaky, you could sit down or lean against a wall, observe what's going on in your body and what your mind is telling you, and then ride out the storm as you did in Chapter 22. Then you'd get up and buy your daughter the shoes you promised her.

In both scenarios, you're doing something. And your choice of actions, in a very real sense, helps define who you are and what your life is about. The next imagery exercise will help you connect with this basic truth.

THE POWER TO CHOOSE

Imagine you're driving through life on a long road toward a mountain—let's call it your "value mountain." It stands for everything you care about in life, and what you want to be about as a person. This is where you want to go.

So there you are, driving happily along, and suddenly anxiety jumps out and blocks the road. You hit the brakes and quickly turn right to avoid a collision. But now you find yourself on the emotional "control-and-avoidance" detour. This detour has its own road. Like a roundabout or a rotary, it goes in circles. So you go round and round, waiting, hoping for anxiety to pass. Meanwhile, your life ticks by.

This is what happens when you struggle with your unpleasant thoughts and feelings. You feel stuck, going in circles, and far from the life you really want. You don't want your life to be about driving on the control-and-avoidance detour. And yet it's so easy to get stuck there. Many people do.

But you don't have to remain there. You can change how you respond to anxiety and fear. Instead of turning away, you can stay on the road toward your values and bring anxiety and fear along with you. No longer reacting or struggling, you choose to drive forward with them because choosing the old alternative costs you.

The first and most important task is to make a choice to move forward when anxiety tries to block your path. The second is to be willing to take what you're thinking and feeling with you as you move forward. Unless you do both, you'll continue to remain stuck.

The cumulative effect of your choices and your actions determines what your life will become. Everything you do from here on out adds up to that. How you choose and what you do creates your destiny and legacy. This is the prize!

29 Discover Your Passions

What matters to you? Do you really know? If not, now is the time to find out.

We all have a finite amount of time on this earth. Sadly, many of us plow through each day on autopilot, never stopping to take a good hard look at what we're spending our time doing or asking ourselves, "Is this truly what I want to be about?" Most people don't think about it until it's too late to do something about it. Don't let that happen to you.

We all know that death is inevitable. Most of us have no control over when or how we'll die. But we can control how we live from this day forward.

Firsthand accounts teach us that something profound happens when people have been near death and have survived to live another day. Facing death forces people to wake up and take stock. Priorities are rearranged. Old habits and activities that once seemed so important become trivial. Instead, time, energy, and resources are poured into doing things that really matter. These activities are what they (and you) will be remembered for.

The following are two related journaling exercises that'll help you connect with what you want your life to stand for. The exercises may seem a bit strange and scary, but they're also very powerful. Take your time with them.

ANXIETY-MANAGEMENT EPITAPH

Your task here is to write your epitaph (the inscription on your gravestone) as it would be written if you were to die today. What would it say if it was about what you've been doing to manage your anxiety? What have you become by living in service of your anxiety? Bring to mind all of the coping and management strategies you use to keep anxiety and fear at bay. Be mindful of how they've gotten in the way of what you want to do. Think of all the things you say aloud, think to yourself, or do with your hands or feet before, during, or after anxiety shows up. If you like, you can get out a piece of paper and list them all.

This exercise asks you to face squarely what your life has become in service of not being anxious or afraid. We understand that this exercise is probably difficult, perhaps even a bit depressing to do. But the next exercise should be more uplifting.

We'd like you to write another epitaph, but this time as you'd really like it to read, without the stains of anxiety and fear having taken up all of your time and energy. This epitaph embodies everything you truly care about and wish to be known for. This is your *Valued Life Epitaph*!

VALUED LIFE EPITAPH

Imagine that you could live your life free of any struggle with worry, anxiety, or fear. Wouldn't that be something? What would you do? What would you want to be about?

As you connect with this, imagine that you're standing in front of the headstone on your grave. Right away you notice it's blank. Your epitaph (words describing your life) hasn't been written yet. What inscription would you like to see on your headstone?

Think of a phrase or series of brief statements that would capture the essence of the life you want to lead. What do you want to be remembered for? What would you be doing with your time and energy?

Give yourself some time to think about these really important questions. If you find an answer—or more than one—write them down. There are no limits to what you can be remembered for. Think big.

This isn't a hypothetical exercise, either. What you'll be remembered for, what defines your life, is up to you. It depends on what you do now. It depends on the actions you take. This is how you determine the wording of your epitaph.

When you're finished, compare your *Valued Life Epitaph* with your *Anxiety-Management Epitaph*. Which epitaph do you want to be known for? Which one is more life affirming and true to the person you want to be?

We understand that getting a handle on anxiety is important to you, but do you really want your tombstone to read, "Here lies [your name]—who finally got rid of anxiety"? If that inscription doesn't excite you, you're in good company. We've done this exercise with countless people just like you. And we've never seen anyone write something like that.

What does it mean when people never mention anxiety on tombstones or eulogies? Perhaps getting rid of your anxiety—a goal you've been working so hard to achieve— isn't going to matter much in the grand scheme of things. Every sixty seconds you spend trying to get a handle on your anxiety is a minute taken away from doing something that matters to you.

In short, the anxiety struggle pulls you out of your life. If you're not doing things to be the type of person you want to be, now is the time to live the life you want and do the things that are most important to you. It's time to choose your valued life.

30 Finding Your North Star

For thousands of years, navigators have relied on the North Star to help guide them on their journeys. They've been taught how to locate it easily in the night sky and to use it wisely. And many still rely on the North Star to this very day.

Instead of looking upward to the stars for guidance, you can learn to bring your awareness back to earth, relying on your values to guide you. Just as the night sky appears to rotate around the North Star, your values are the point around which your life turns. Values offer each one of us a sense of direction, meaning, and purpose. When life appears stormy and difficult, your values will help you navigate a way forward. Without a clear sense of what matters, you'll end up making choices that leave you feeling directionless, lost, and without hope.

So knowing your values is an important step in creating the kind of life you wish to live and the kind of person you wish to become. Once you get clear about what truly matters, then you can draw on your values and turn to them as your abiding North Star, always pointing you to what's truly important in your life.

MY NORTH STAR(S)

- Imagine you could spend your time doing anything. In your mind, ask yourself, "If _____ [insert anxiety- or fear-related concern, or anything else you struggle with here] wasn't such a problem for me, then what would I be doing? _____ [insert your answer here].

- When you've determined what you'd be doing, open your eyes and write it down in a word or two.

- What does this activity represent for you? Perhaps it's freedom? Or a greater sense of connection with other people? Or maybe it's creativity, family, expression, learning, growth, and so on. Listen to your heart for the answer!

- Capture the essence of the activity in a single word. This is your North Star.

Repeat the exercise as often as you like, but five to ten times usually works well. Come back to it on another day if you like. Each time you repeat the exercise, think about something new you would be doing with your time, and then a new word or two that captures the essence of that activity in terms of your values. Once you've cycled through this exercise several times, you'll end up with a list of your values. No need to rush. It's better to linger with this one and listen to your heart, your deepest longings and desires.

31 Opening the Right Doors

When we speak of valuing, we're talking about two things. First, what matters to you and only you! And second, what you do to express this in your life. The second piece is critical, because your values find expression in your actions—in what you do with your mouth, hands, and feet.

So, for example, you may believe that you should be a good parent, but without any actions, your belief is just that—a bunch of thoughts swirling around in your head. If you want to bring your values to life, then you'll need to look at your actions in your role as a parent. You might even ask, "What do I want to be about as a parent? What does that look like?" Likewise, if you're someone who believes in helping others, you need to act in ways that are helpful. If you don't act out your values, they're just empty beliefs. Beliefs or morality without action are empty vessels. They may look good, but otherwise they are of no consequence.

As you consider your own values, you'll need to allow yourself time to think about areas of your life that are deeply important to you, and what you want to be about as a person. These are the qualities of expression that make your life worth living, that you want to cherish and nurture, and that you'd act to defend if necessary.

HOMING IN ON IMPORTANT VALUES

Refer to the North Stars you identified in the previous chapter. You'll know when you're homing in on an important value of yours if you can answer yes to each of the following questions:

1. Do I care about [insert North Star word]?

2. Am I doing this for me? If nobody knew, would I still care about it? Or, am I doing this because I'm supposed to, or because that's what others want me to do, or so people approve of me?

3. Can I control and do this—take action—myself? (Keep in mind that what other people say and do is not in your control.)

4. Does it have the potential to bring me joy, contentment, and a sense of vitality and satisfaction? (Values ought be rewarding at some level, even if you encounter difficulties along the way.)

5. Is this something that I cannot put on a to-do list and be done with it? (Values are more like a journey, not a destination where you arrive and that's the end of it.)

6. Am I willing to act in ways to express my values, even knowing that I may not always get what I want?

Life is energy—and this energy is a precious gift. You can choose to focus that energy on whatever is important to you. Or you can squander it on things that, in the end, pull you out of your life. Your values will help guide you here. So take time to reflect on what matters to you and the kind of life you wish to lead from this point onward. As you do, keep this question in mind: How can I use my time and energy wisely? This is something you can do!

32 Making Wise Choices

The serenity creed reminds us to accept what cannot be changed while at the same time encouraging us to change what can be changed. The only prerequisite is that we be willing to experience what is. There is enormous wisdom in this teaching. That is why people love it so much. But it also contains the seeds of enormous frustration. How can we know what can and cannot be changed?

By now, you're probably coming to the realization that you don't have a great deal of control over anxiety. Your experience tells you as much. And your experience is right on.

But you can choose what you do with anxiety. You can choose to open up and soften to your experience of anxiety, or any other inner experience that you tend to struggle with. You can choose willingness, because willingness is what you can control and change. It is the key that will unlock many doors, opening you to the possibility of living a vital and meaningful life more fearlessly and without fear controlling you. The next imagery exercise will help you connect with this truth.

WILLINGNESS CREATES POSSIBILITIES

Imagine you have two switches in front of you. They look like light switches; each appears to have an on-off setting. One switch is called "anxiety" and the other is called "willingness." When you started reading this book, you were probably hoping to find a way to turn off the anxiety switch, but this turned out to be a false hope. The on-off toggle of the anxiety switch isn't working—it never has and probably never will. And you don't have to trust us. Just look at your experience. Nobody has the power to flip the anxiety switch off, whether temporarily or permanently.

Here we'd like to share a secret with you. The willingness switch is really the more important of the two, because it's the one that will make a difference in your life. Unlike the anxiety switch, the willingness switch actually works, and you can and do control this switch. Your emotions will rise and fall more or less on their own. But regardless of your emotional weather, you can always decide to turn on your willingness switch.

When it comes to willingness, you're not a help-less victim, because that switch is controlled by your actions, your behavior. This is the place where you are *response-able*, or able to do some-thing. It's your choice to flip the willingness switch on or off.

We're not sure what would happen with your anxiety if you switched willingness on. But we do know this: You really *can* switch it on if you make a choice to do so. And then things might start to happen in your life. You could start doing what you really want to do and start moving in the direction of your *Valued Life Epitaph*.

Please be mindful that we're not talking about ignoring anxiety with the willingness switch. We're simply encourag-ing you to shift your attention from what you cannot control to what you can control.

33 Do, No Trying

"I'll try" is one of the first things people tell us when they talk about choosing willingness. But this is a recipe for staying stuck. You may even tell yourself "I'll try" too when thinking about the next time you're anxious. You may think, "I'll really try to be willing and not do what I usually do." And when things don't work out, you may tell yourself, "I tried to go to work. I tried really hard, but I just couldn't do it. My anxiety was just too strong. So I stayed home."

The following brief exercise is a powerful way for you to connect with the fact that willingness is an all-or-nothing action. Either you do it or you don't. There's no trying to do something. There's no trying to be willing either.

THE TRYING PEN

Have a seat at a table and place a pen in front of you. Now, we'd like you to try to pick up the pen. Try as hard as you can. Go ahead and try it. If you find yourself picking up the pen, stop! That isn't what we asked you to do. We want you to *try* to pick it up.

After some effort, you're probably thinking, "Well, I can't do that. Either I pick it up or I don't." You're right. There's no way to try to pick up the pen and at the same time actually pick it up.

You may have noticed that your hand was stuck hovering over the pen when you tried to pick it up. That's what trying gets you. You end up hovering over things in your life and not doing what you wish to do—like when you try to lose weight, try to get more exercise, try to do a better job, try to be a better lover, try to be a more responsive parent, try to be more organized, try to be a better listener, or try to be less anxious. Trying just leaves you hovering, in a state of paralysis, and stuck.

Trying is really a form of "not doing." You must first make a choice about whether you're willing to do something. If you are completely willing rather than just a bit willing, then go ahead and do it. And if you aren't willing, then don't do it. Remember, willingness has an on-off switch, not some type of dial you can move up or down a little.

Responsibility for flipping your willingness switch rests with you. It's time to face this stark truth squarely. Your behavior is something you can control—even when you're in the grip of powerful emotions like anxiety and fear. This is good news.

You don't have to *feel willing* in order to *act with willingness*. That's because willingness isn't a feeling. So when we encourage you to be willing, we aren't asking you to change how you feel. You can still think that your anxieties are unpleasant and dislike them. With willingness, we're asking you to make a choice. That choice is to be with your anxieties when they show up and do what matters to you.

34 Exercise Kindness

Many people are troubled by difficult emotions and thoughts but lack the skills to deal with them. They think that the best thing to do is to fight back. This natural inclination is a source of needless suffering.

A far more effective and skillful way to approach any harsh energy is to meet it with loving-kindness. This means that you treat your mind and body with friendliness, gentleness, equanimity, and, dare we say it, love. When you do that, emotional pain and suffering will have no room to grow and take over your life.

Kindness itself is simple and yet hard for most people. But don't let that stop you. You can learn to be kind with yourself. Just as people work out to build muscle, your kindness muscle requires regular use and practice. This muscle will grow stronger over time. You can start building your kindness muscle daily whenever you find yourself walking.

This next exercise builds on the *Mindful Walking* practice you did earlier (see Chapter 13), but with an important twist. The twist involves walking with loving-kindness in your mind and heart.

WALKING WITH LOVING-KINDNESS

For this practice, all you need to do is walk at a normal pace, inside or outside. As you walk, silently repeat a meaningful phrase or mantra—one that reflects a loving-kindness intention and wish for yourself. Keep it simple—such as "May I have peace," "May I be kind to myself," "May I experience joy," or "May I be free of needless suffering." Listen to your heart.

Before moving on, come up with your own personal phrase:

"May I _____."

As you walk and move, silently repeat your personal loving-kindness phrase. When something or someone outside of you grabs your attention, notice what it is, and then silently extend your personal phrase to that object, person, or creature. So, if a tree catches your attention, you would silently extend your phrase to that tree—for example, "May this tree have peace." If it's a stranger, do the same. If it's a memory, thought, or feeling, do the same. If it's an animal, car, or some other object, do the same. If this seems odd or strange, that's okay. Just continue extending the phrase to anything that catches your attention.

Then, after you silently extend your personal loving-kindness phrase to whatever grabbed your attention, bring your awareness back to yourself, and continue to walk as you repeat your kindness mantra silently to yourself ("May I..."). Repeat this process of extending your phrase to yourself and then to anything that pulls your attention and back to yourself for as long as you wish.

When you face difficulty in your daily life, this practice is a simple and empowering way to soften the blows. Start with making a daily intention to practice when you're walking, and then when you find yourself sitting or waiting in line. Do the practice with an open mind, and let go of any attachment to getting a specific outcome. Over time and with practice, loving-kindness will become more of a habit in your daily life.

35 Don't Feed It

Everything you've been learning and practicing up to this point is to prepare you to *live* your life when life gets hard, and especially when you feel anxious or afraid. That's because you're different now. You're armed with a new perspective that'll help you create the kind of life you wish to live, anxiety or not. But that doesn't mean you won't be pulled into old ways. The trick is to learn how not to feed anxiety and fear when and if they do show up, because they probably will.

Think of your anxieties as a hungry tiger cub, a pet that lives with you in your home. She's so cute, but a little bit scary too. So, to keep the tiger happy, you make sure she gets lots of meat. And you keep feeding her and feeding her, wanting to keep her happy. But deep down you're also scared that she might bite you, or worse, see you as dinner.

Each time you feed her, she quiets down and leaves you alone for a bit. But over time, she grows, and grows, and grows. Now she's not so cute. She's loud, difficult to manage, and always hungry. In fact, she's frightening.

But you keep feeding her. And while she eats, she leaves you alone. But she keeps growing. Back and forth, over and over, the same drama plays itself out. You hope that one day she'll finally leave you alone and for good.

Yet the tiger doesn't leave—she just gets louder and scarier and hungrier. And then one day you walk to the fridge, you open the door, and the fridge is empty. At this point, there's nothing left to feed to the tiger—nothing, except *you!*

The lesson here is simple. When you're faced with your anxiety tiger, don't feed it. Stop doing what you've always done. Instead, do something radically different from what you've done before! That's it.

But we also know that simple doesn't mean easy. You might even be thinking, "Well, that's all well and good, but how do I do that?" Here are a few bits of advice to help tame your tiger of anxiety and fear so it doesn't consume you.

TAMING THE ANXIETY TIGER

1. Choose what you attend to and do. Everything else pivots on this one. You can choose to attend to and listen to what the anxiety tiger tells you, and to do as it says. Or you can choose to watch all the activity from an observer perspective, without buying into it, and act with your mouth, hands, and feet, guided by your values. Remember, anxiety is a part of you, but there's much more to you and your life than that.

2. **Acknowledge what's happening anyway.**
    Anxiety happens. Remember that it's not a
    choice. But you do have a choice in how you
    respond to it. You can choose to feed it or
    you can choose to get curious about it, open
    up to it, and let it be. Like waves on the ocean,
    it will pass.

3. **Do the opposite of what anxiety compels you
    to do.** When the anxiety tiger tells you to stay
    put, sitting on your hands, you get up. When
    you're compelled to turn away, you get curious
    and lean in. When you're inclined to freeze,
    you move. When you feel like you're losing
    touch or you find yourself lost in the past or
    future, you take a rich grounding breath and
    bring your awareness back to where you are
    right now. When you find yourself agitated,
    you allow yourself to sit still with the energy
    inside. As you've learned before, doing the
    opposite of what your anxieties and fears
    command is a powerful way to take back
    control over your life.

4. **Be kind and gentle with yourself.** Above all,
    practice being gentle with yourself. This is
    not the time to start another tug-of-war with

your anxiety. In a way, being gentle and kind is the exact opposite of warfare. This is why it can be so powerful. Just don't use it as a clever way to make the anxiety go away. If you do that, you'll likely just find yourself right back where you started and caught in another war, except using a new set of weapons. The kindness exercises you're learning in this book will help you develop a new relationship with your mind, body, and experience.

We realize it can be difficult to leave your old ways behind and adopt a new approach. But here's the deal: You're the master and creator of your life. The anxiety tiger has no power unless you feed her and give her that power. This is one place where you can take control and make a real difference in your life.

36 Body Surfing Emotions

When waves approach a group of birds floating on the water, you'll notice that the birds don't fly away. They bob up and down as they ride up the facing slope, round the top, and drift down the long backside of the wave. You can learn to do this with your anxieties too.

All emotions are wavelike and time limited. They ebb and flow like waves—they build up, eventually reach a peak, and drift away. Anxiety and fear come and go in a similar way. They don't last forever, even if it feels as if they will.

When you're experiencing strong emotions, the waves are tall and scary. You may feel that they'll go on forever and overwhelm you, or that you may drown. But that's the old anxiety talking. You decide not to listen, and just keep on riding.

Like the birds on the water, you can simply stay and do nothing. That may seem impossible, but you can still choose to stay and do the opposite of what your anxiety is commanding you to do. We know how difficult this is without some experiential practice on your part.

So we encourage you to do the following exercise to prepare you for challenging moments when you're faced with anxiety waves. In your mind and with your imagination, right now you have a chance to learn to stay on the wave of your anxiety and fear, ride it out, and see what happens.

RIDING THE WAVES

- Think of a recent situation when you felt afraid, panicky, nervous, worried, or upset. Visualize the scene and remember how you felt. Pause for a while.

- Keep focusing on the upsetting scene and imagine that it's an ocean wave as it approaches you near the shoreline. It looks far too big for you and is very scary. Notice the worry, disconcerting thoughts, and maybe images of disaster too. Keep focusing on the upsetting scene as well as on the judgments you make about it, about you, and about what's happening inside you.

- Now observe what your body might be doing. Notice the sensations and how your mind evaluates them. Simply label them all: "I am noticing _____." Notice the sensations of warmth and of tightness. Just let your body and mind do their thing.

- Do the same with worries, other thoughts, and images that show up—the old story line. Acknowledge their presence without trying to control them, change them, or push them away. Label them and keep watching your mind and body.

- Be aware of the point where your anxiety wave stops climbing. It has reached its peak, weakens, and starts to recede. You feel the wave leveling off and starting to diminish. Experience the slow ride down the back of the wave. Accept wherever you are on the wave. Don't try to get past it. It moves at its own speed. Just let go and let it carry you. Eventually, you'll feel yourself slipping down the back of the wave, the anxiety now quieting.

Anxiety and fear work just like a wave if you don't try to control or block them. But if you refuse to face and ride out the wave, it'll throw you back and toss you around like a beach ball. Then you're caught churning helplessly beneath the surface of the water, at the mercy of the full force of the crushing wave and undertow.

But if you swim or ride with the waves, or at least not against them, they'll eventually carry you toward the safe shore. The same will happen if you stop fighting your anxiety waves.

37 Refocus, Reconnect, and Redirect

If you've ever been around a child throwing a tantrum, you know how unsettling that can be. In the heat of the moment, it's so easy to lose focus, your connection with yourself and other people around you, and even your sense of direction. Anxiety can leave you feeling like that too. You're at your wits' end and want it to stop.

With the tantrum, you may have a great urge to respond in anger or with harshness. But this, we know, often makes things worse. In fact, countless studies teach us that these strategies are poor ways to encourage more appropriate behaviors in children. Parents end up feeling bad, tired, and frustrated. Worse, the kids grow up fearing their parents and end up being very hard on themselves and others too.

Other parents and caregivers opt for a more compassionate, yet firm, approach. They *refocus* and see their child as part of them, not as some alien monster.

Then they move past that first impulse to react with negative energy and punishing behavior, and they *reconnect* with what they want to be about in this situation. Most parents wish for their children to be safe and secure, and to know kindness and love, so they do their best to respond in ways that show that.

But they don't just let the kids run the show. They *redirect* behavior, taking their child in directions the parents want to go and in directions that are best for the child, too.

Research shows that learning to refocus, reconnect, and redirect is a highly effective parenting strategy and a powerful way to find peace during difficulty. You can learn to do the same when your anxiety acts out too. The next exercise will help you do this.

TRAVELING WITH MY ANXIETY CHILD

Imagine that your anxiety is more like a child— your child—acting out again, throwing a fit. Think about how you normally respond. What's your parenting strategy? Do you yell, scream, and struggle? If you do, has it worked? Or do you end up feeling worse—frustrated and tired out by the constant nagging? Does your anxiety child respond well to that or continue to act up? Now let's see what happens as you refocus, reconnect, and redirect.

Refocus—Take a rich grounding breath in and let it slowly out. Now look at this anxiety child of yours and notice that this child is part of you and not you. See if you can look past the negative energy, and see that your anxiety child is looking to you, and only you, for some guidance and care. You know what's best for this child—and for you too.

Reconnect—Your anxiety child may be hurting and in need of your comfort. Connect with what you'd like to be about in this situation. Do you want to approach your anxiety child with a declaration of war in hand? Or can you reconnect with your anxiety and fear from a place of gentleness, compassion, and kindness? This doesn't mean you like what your anxiety child is doing. It means that you can still treat your anxiety child in a loving way. Do this because ultimately it's good for you.

Redirect—Your anxiety child is probably demanding and wants you to stay put or avoid a situation. But you are the one in charge. This is your life. So, in a firm and loving way, you decide to take your anxiety child with you as you do something that matters to you. Your anxiety child may protest, but this is your life. You have the power to choose what you do and where you go. Your anxiety child doesn't have that power unless you give the child that power.

Perhaps it's time to refocus, reconnect, and redirect. After all, your anxiety child is a part of you. You can be firm and respond with kindness and love. This is how you cultivate a loving home within yourself so you don't get sidetracked when your anxiety child acts out. The next time you go out to do something you care about, if your anxiety child decides to show up, say "Come along with me."

38 Moving with Barriers

As you embark on your journey, you'll find the road full of barriers. Some barriers are external, such as lack of money, competing life demands on your time and resources, limited opportunities, physical or geographical constraints, or even foul weather. You can work through some of these barriers by brainstorming options or by talking with a good friend to get some perspective and fresh ideas. Yet by far the most frequent and tricky barriers that you'll face are those nagging, pesky anxiety- and fear-related thoughts, feelings, bodily sensations, or impulses that have slowed you down in the past.

Your mind will tell you that when a barrier comes up, you should just get rid of it—overcome it. The problem with this strategy is that it awakens your natural inclination to struggle. You know by now that struggling with anxiety and fear doesn't work well. So when a barrier comes up, you need to listen to and trust your experience, not your mind!

The good news is that you don't need to get rid of anxiety barriers on your road to living your values. You don't need to push them aside either. There's no healthy way to do that anyway. The key is to move *with* the barriers—take them along for the ride! This is the path to living fearlessly.

You can deal with any anxiety obstacle in the same way that you deal with other thoughts and feelings: You make room for all the unwanted stuff that has been stopping you from doing what's best for you. You acknowledge that stuff and watch it from your observer perspective. Above all, you let it be, without getting involved with it, and keep on moving in the direction you want to go—all at the same time. The next imagery exercise will help you get in touch with what we mean.

WHO'S DRIVING YOUR "LIFE BUS"?

Think of yourself as the driver of a bus called "My Life." Imagine that you're headed north toward your Value Mountain, _____ [insert one of your important values here].

Along the way, you pick up some unruly passengers, like frightening thoughts and images that your mind comes up with. Other passengers may take the form of tension and feelings of apprehension and panic. These passengers are loud, persistent, and scary. They try to bully you as you drive along your chosen route. They shout, "Don't go there! It's too dangerous. You'll make a fool of yourself. You'll never be happy. STO-O-OPPPPP!"

You try to come up with arguments and strategies to quiet them. Distracted, you realize that you missed a road sign and took a wrong turn. Now you're an hour out of your way, headed south. You are, in a very real sense, lost. So you stop the bus and focus on getting your passengers in line. This time you turn around, face them, and let them have it: "Why can't you leave me alone? I'm sick of you. Just give me a few moments to relax."

Look at what's happened here. You've stopped the bus, let go of the steering wheel, and turned yourself around, and your eyes are looking at the back of the bus instead of the road ahead and your real destination. You're not moving. Instead, you're paying attention to the stuff that has nothing to do with your values.

Here you're faced with another choice. You can stay tangled up in arguments and strategies to calm the passengers, or you can let them be, get back in the driver's seat, turn on the engine, grab the steering wheel, and find your way back onto the road toward your Value Mountain.

If moving toward what you care about is important to you, then you need to stay in the driver's seat of your Life Bus at all times. The unpleasant passengers will still be in the bus with you. You can't kick them off. While you're driving your Life Bus on the road to your Value Mountain, every now and then the passengers will creep forward and scream, "Pay attention to us! Turn around! Go back! Take this detour—it's safer, easier, and it'll make you feel better."

Once again, you must make a choice. What will you do? Stopping won't get you to the mountain; neither will the detour. Only you can take yourself to where you want to go—and you have no choice but to take all the passengers with you. Thoughts and feelings cannot prevent you from continuing toward where you want to go. That is, unless you give them that power.

The passengers on your Life Bus are not all dark and menacing. In fact, if you listen closely you may notice the voices of other passengers who are desperately trying to be heard. These are the voices of your values. They've been drowned out and ignored until now, but if you stay in your driver's seat and listen, you'll hear them. They will remind you of the good that you're doing for your life each time you stay in the driver's seat and move your bus in directions that matter to you!

Your anxious and fearful passengers will grab every opportunity to steer you off course. They'll try to convince you that you don't feel like doing this anymore, that it's all too much, too difficult, not worth it. Even then, you can still choose to keep on moving toward what matters to you. You can't control what kinds of feelings, thoughts, or fears ride along with you. But you can control where your Life Bus is going—you control the steering wheel with your hands and the accelerator and brakes with your feet. Don't forget that!

39 Lay Off the But(t)s

At some point you've probably said something like "I'd like to go out, *but* I'm afraid of having a panic attack, embarrassing myself, or getting anxious." Snap—you just got caught in the "yes, but" trap.

Anytime you put "but" after the first part of a statement, you undo and negate what you just said. This is the literal meaning of the word "but." This common word also sets up your anxieties and fears as barriers and problems you need to resolve before you take action. Let's see how this plays out with an example.

So when you say, "I'd like to go out, *but* I'm afraid of having a panic attack," you "undo" your interest in going out—and then you won't go out. You'll stay home, because that "but" negates the "like to go out."

"But" also sets you up for struggle. Either the liking to go out has to go away or the fear of having a panic attack has to go away. This is why when you use "buts" often, you'll end up quite literally stuck on your butt. "But" makes going out or doing much of anything impossible.

If you pay close attention, you may find that you use the word "but" many times every day as a reason for not acting on your values. This unnecessarily restricts your life, holds you back, and reduces your options.

The next exercise will help you catch your "yes, but" traps.

THE "YES, BUT(T)" TRAP

Take a moment to reflect on times when you found yourself thinking about something you'd really like to do and then, in the next breath, following that with "but." For instance, "I'd really like to go to the party, but I might be uncomfortable and do something stupid." See if you can come up with at least three situations in which there was something you'd like to do followed by "but [insert what normally comes to mind]." Write them down.

Now, cross out the "but" in each statement and replace it with the word "and." Read the statement again. Do it slowly. Does it feel any different with "and" instead of "but"? It should.

This little change can have a dramatic impact on what might happen next. You could go to the party and be uncomfortable with your mind telling you that you might say something stupid. Using "and" instead of "but" allows you to do something vital and feel anxious. It gives you more choice and freedom. It's also a more honest expression of what's really going on for you in the moment.

Starting today, every time a "but" is about to keep you stuck on your butt, practice saying "and" instead of "but." As you do that, bring your awareness to new opportunities that open up for you. Getting off your but(t)s could be one of the most empowering things you've ever done.

40 Unhooking from the Past

It's very easy to get hooked on the past. Everyone collects painful moments like rain droplets falling into a bucket. When you look into your life bucket, you probably have things that you'd rather dump out, as well as pleasant moments that you cling to and want to keep around.

Maybe what's in your bucket includes combat, or an accident, a rape, loss, abuse, regrets, missed opportunities, or choices that you wish you could undo. It may be a difficult childhood, or anger and resentment at how your parents and friends treated you. Wonderful past experiences may also linger, and you may feel loss and sadness about the fact that they're missing from your life now. It's all in the mix.

These experiences may have left a deep mark on you then, and they still do now. Each time you remember, you're propelled back to the hurt, the anger, and the loss, and you may sink deep into an overwhelming sense of guilt or shame.

There's absolutely nothing wrong with being able to remember the good, bad, and ugly moments you've lived through. Without that ability, you wouldn't learn and grow. And it's okay that you don't like remembering some of your past. Everyone has had experiences they'd rather forget.

Some have had it worse than others. Yet everyone has had something.

But getting hooked on the past and dwelling there is a trap. The next imagery exercise will show you why.

STUCK STIRRING
A BUCKET OF SHIT!

Imagine that you're sitting next to a large bucket that holds everything from your past. You try to resist opening the lid, but for whatever reason, the lid pops off. Curious, you look into the bucket and see that it's full of shit, and it really smells awful. So you grab a large wooden spoon and start stirring, hoping that this might somehow dissolve it and lessen the smell.

In a way, getting hooked on the past is like getting caught stirring a bucket of shit, around and around, again and again, with your mind telling you, "You can't go forward because of the pain you lived through." Or "You don't deserve to go forward." It might even say, "If you stir long enough, you'll figure this out, and it will all go away." So you keep stirring, going back, reopening old wounds, regrets, painful experiences.

Maybe you think that if you stir long enough, something will change. But truthfully, no amount of stirring will turn shit into sweet ice cream.

Here's something else to notice—all of this remembering, reliving, and stirring is happening right now, in the present. There's no time machine to go back in. Time only goes forward, and you have to go forward too.

What's needed here is for you to acknowledge the past as the past, let go of the spoon, and drop all the unhelpful stories your mind baits you with. Then you'll be able to focus on where you are, right now, what you want to do, right *now*, and where you want to go in your life, right *now*.

From the present, you can learn to notice remembering for what it is—your mind thinking—and then meet that experience with gentle curiosity and kindness. That's how to free yourself from your mind's attachments to the past, and all of its traps and snares.

This isn't about forgetting or condoning the wrongs or challenges you endured. Instead, you decide to learn from them, open up to them, honor them, and carry them forward in ways that dignify your life right now.

So if you're willing, make the choice to stop stirring. Then, with your mind and hands free, choose what you'd like to spend your time doing from this moment forward.

41 Grounding in the Now

When a painful or traumatic memory pops into your aware-ness, it's easy to get pulled out of the present in a flash. When this happens, the first thing you need to do is pause, take a few slow deep breaths, and notice what's happening. You're remembering, which is just another form of thinking. And notice that you're doing it now, from the safe refuge of the present.

We know that this can seem hard at first. If you tend to get lost in a whirlwind of thoughts about your past, or find that the trauma you've endured seems to pull you out of the present or even right out of your body—like you're in another place—then you know what losing your sense of grounding feels like. It's like having the rug pulled out from under you. That can be scary, and it makes it hard to be right where you are and do what matters.

Here's an exercise that will help you ground yourself wherever you are and regain your ground when you've been snared by thoughts from your past. All you need for this exercise is about five minutes. Read the exercise a few times and then practice it yourself.

USING YOUR FIVE SENSES

When you feel like you're losing your ground, you can use any of your five senses—taste, smell, touch, sight, and hearing—to ground yourself in the present once more. For maximum benefit, it's best to engage your senses intensely and fully as you do this grounding practice anywhere you find yourself.

Engage each of your senses as best you can:

- **Taste** something that's strong, like a lemon or black coffee.

- **Smell** something that's pungent, like cologne, fresh herbs, soap, or your pet's fur.

- **Touch** objects that have unique textures, shapes, or weight.

- **Look** at something bright, stark, or unusual—a picture or something in your field of vision.

- **Listen**, focusing on sounds that stand out in your environment.

Engaging your senses this way brings you back to the present. Just be mindful about why you're doing this. It's easy to use your senses as a clever way to turn away from painful memories, but that just puts your memories in charge and gives them more power to steer your life off track. Instead, engage your senses with your life in mind—as a way to come back to the *now* so that you can act on your life and values now.

As you practice these grounding strategies, see what works best for you. As you do, remind yourself that you are here in the now—present, alert, and alive.

Practice this exercise, eyes closed or open, as often as you can, wherever you are. Grounding in the now will help you stay present and give you skills to regain your ground when you find yourself being pulled into your past by a difficult memory. Grounding is also a useful way to show up to your life and live your values right where you are.

42 Releasing Attachments

Pain is a natural and normal part of living well. When you shut down to pain, you shut down to life. When you open up to life, you must open up to pain in all its forms. This is how it works. To have it all, you must be willing to have it *all*—the good, neutral, unpleasant, and sometimes ugly.

You can learn a powerful way to open up to difficulty: you simply stop both avoiding pain and chasing pleasure. You invite in the discomfort you're feeling anyway and give away what's good and joyful. You breathe in the discomfort and receive it, then breathe out and away what you so desperately want and think will bring relief.

If you let the words go—loosen your attachment to the story line—and just feel the discomfort and sit with it without getting tangled up with it, you share what we all share. That's what compassion really means. Experiencing this sense of shared humanity has tremendous healing power—it's the path out of misery and into vitality.

Breathing in pain and breathing out relief is the basis of an ancient form of meditation called *tonglen* (meaning "giving and receiving"). Welcoming your pain and giving away good may seem backward. But that's precisely why it can be so powerful.

When you embrace what you don't like, you transform it. That very act is an acknowledgment that you share what we all share—the very real and human capacity to hurt. When you give to others what you so desperately seek for yourself, you become empowered. That transformation will release you from your attachment to "feeling better" and your resistance to fear and other unpleasant emotions. Above all, it will nurture your capacity for love and compassion. The next exercise will help you develop these important skills.

EMBRACING THE "BAD," GIVING AWAY THE "GOOD"

Start by getting yourself comfortable in a place where you'll be undisturbed for five to ten minutes. Sit upright with your feet flat on the floor, your arms and legs uncrossed, and your hands resting in your lap.

Now close your eyes and gently guide your attention to the natural rhythm of your breath in your chest and belly. After a few moments, bring to mind something painful or hurtful, perhaps a recent event or a time when you felt very anxious. Then, with your next inhale, visualize taking in that negativity and painful upset. As you fill your lungs with the discomfort, be mindful that what you're feeling in this very moment is being felt by millions of people all over this world. You're not alone with this. Countless people have felt this anxiety since the dawn of time.

Your intention here, for yourself and others, is for you and them to be free of the suffering, the struggle, blame, and any shame associated with the pain that you and they experience. With that intention in mind, on each exhale, breathe out relief, joyfulness, and goodwill. Do it slowly with the natural rhythm of your breathing. Continue to connect with your pain as you breathe in, and with each exhale extend goodwill and a wish that others may find relief from the suffering they get caught in when they experience hurt and discomfort.

If you find breathing in anxiety gets too heavy or tight, you can imagine breathing into a vast space. In fact, your heart is such a vast space, and you can make it even bigger. Imagine breathing into your heart, making it bigger and bigger with every inhale until there's enough space for all the worries, anxieties, and concerns. With each exhale, you're opening up your whole being so you no longer have to push away anxiety or fear—you're opening your heart to whatever arises.

If you find your mind wandering or you feel distracted, just kindly notice that and come back to the intention of welcoming in your pain and hurts, and releasing goodwill and kindness. Continue this practice of giving and receiving for as long as you wish.

Then, when you're ready, gradually widen your attention and gently open your eyes with the intention of giving and receiving throughout the day.

When you notice yourself getting anxious and wanting to climb out of your skin, you can practice on-the-spot tonglen for all the people out there who, just like you, get caught in the struggle by pushing their discomfort away when they notice it. Right then, wherever you are, you can breathe in, acknowledge the discomfort, and breathe out a sense of peace and calm for yourself and everyone else going through the same experience. Every moment you're willing to stay with uncomfortable anxiety, you're learning more and more not to fear it.

43 Drifting Along

Psychologists estimate that human beings have sixty thousand to eighty thousand thoughts each day. But we attend to very few of them. The ones we do pay attention to tend to stick around and can needlessly limit our lives. What we must learn is to allow our thoughts to come and go, because they will, if we let them.

This practice is important when you find yourself paying attention to anxious thoughts, even urges. The more you attend to these thoughts, the more they will stick around, increasing your anxiety and sense of being stuck. So the practice here is to learn to allow anxious thoughts and urges to come and go without getting entangled with them and without acting on them. This will help you create space between your judgmental mind and your experience.

The next exercise will give you practice watching your thoughts and urges come and go, and not doing what they compel you to do. You'll learn that thoughts really do come and go all by themselves—if you just let them go! The only thing you have to do is watch and wait.

LEAVES ON A STREAM

- Center yourself on your breath as you've done before. Just notice the gentle rising and falling of your breath in your chest and belly. There's no need to control your breathing——simply let the breath breathe itself. Allow your eyes to close gently.

- Then, after a few moments, imagine that you're sitting next to a small stream on a warm autumn day. As you watch the stream, you notice large leaves of all colors, shapes, and sizes drifting along, each at its own pace, one by one, in the slowly moving current. Allow yourself to simply be there for a moment, watching.

- When you're ready, bring your awareness to what's going on inside you. As you do, gently notice and label each experience that shows up—thoughts, feelings, sensations, desires, and impulses. Perhaps one of those thoughts is "I don't have time for this."

- Then, one by one, place each part of your experience on a large leaf passing by. Observe as each leaf comes closer to you. Then watch as it slowly moves away, drifting along as it carries the contents of your mind out of sight downstream. Return to gazing at the stream, waiting for the next leaf to float by. Continue placing each thought, feeling, memory, or impulse on its own large leaf. Watch each one as you let it just float away downstream.

• When you're ready, widen your attention to take in the sounds around you. Open your eyes and make the intention to bring gentle allowing and self-acceptance into the rest of your day.

Practice the *Leaves on a Stream* exercise as often as you can for a couple of weeks. As you get better at it, you can start practicing it during real-life experiences with your eyes open. You can also mix things up a bit by taking the perspective of the stream, just as you took the perspective of the chessboard in the *To Play or Watch the Game?* exercise in Chapter 26. Being the stream, you hold each of the leaves and notice the thought, feeling, sensation, desire, or impulse that each leaf carries as it floats by. Just let them go by and do what they do until they are eventually carried out of sight. And notice how you're learning to be an observer of your experience.

44 Take Good Care

Many of us have old wounds from losses, unfair treatment by others, and, for some, devastating abuse. When painful feelings, images, and memories come up, our first instinctual response often is to push them away. If you catch yourself doing that, please stop. This is a golden opportunity to embrace old hurts with compassion and acceptance.

Why should you do this? People who have been hurt continue to inflict pain on themselves and others because they haven't allowed their wounds to heal. If you don't take care of your wounds, you may pass your pain on to your children, spouse, friends, colleagues, and other people in your life. Hurt can be recycled many times.

To break free from this pattern, you'll have to learn how to take good care of yourself. You do this in the same way you would if you were sick, physically ill, or injured. At those times, you'd probably stop what you were doing and attend to the injury in a kind way. You can do the same with your open anxiety wounds.

Embracing anxiety with compassion is the salve that will help you heal any old wounds that you carry around with you. Compassion teaches us to care for our mind and emotions in the same way as we care for our physical body—with kindness. That's what embracing anxiety with compassion means. You learn to stop being so hard on yourself.

Next is a beautiful exercise that helps you practice self-compassion to take care of your anxieties and fears, or any other form of emotional upset.

HEALING HANDS

Think back to when you were a little child and to a time when you were really sick with a high fever, the flu, or cold symptoms. Notice how you felt really bad. Some adult in your life probably gave you some medicine, and that may have helped a bit. But it was nothing like having your mom or someone else who cared for you there. Reflect on what it felt like when this special person was at your side and put a hand on your forehead. That felt so good!

To you, that hand was like the hand of the divine. This person's hand—or touch—radiated fresh-ness, love, and compassion, and those healing qualities penetrated into your body, your very being. And, for a moment, you felt better. The hand of this special person from your past is still very much alive in your own hand. Let's see what that may be like for you.

Right now, go ahead and close your eyes. Think of a special person or caregiver in your life. And then imagine this person's hand touching you when you were young and sick. Now, touch your forehead or your chest with your hand and see that this caregiver's loving touch is still there. Allow the energy of this special person's loving and tender touch to radiate through your hand and into you. Bring that quality of tenderness to your entire experience.

You can do this exercise by bringing to mind anyone who left you feeling good, loved, and cared for. The kindness of this caring person's hand is alive in yours. And you can give that kindness to yourself, right now and anytime, anywhere.

You can take care of yourself, your anxieties, and your wounds by giving yourself loving-kindness. You don't need to rely on other people to do that for you.

45 Reclaim Your Power

The word "forgiveness" often conjures up a good deal of misunderstanding and confusion. But its essence means nothing more than letting go of a painful past so that you can heal and move on! That's it. And you forgive not to forget, condone, or ignore past wrongs. You forgive because not forgiving virtually guarantees that you'll remain stuck, forever the victim, wanting and waiting for a resolution that may never come. Holding on to past hurts ultimately hurts you, you, you! This is why it needs to stop.

Studies teach us that the willingness to forgive improves health—physical, emotional, and spiritual. Those who learn this important skill report less hurt, stress, anger, depression, and illness. And they get a boost to their energy, hope, optimism, compassion, love, and sense of well-being.

Beyond these benefits, letting go will give you the space to move forward with your life. No longer a prisoner of the injustices of your past, you can chart a new direction for yourself. From this point forward, you decide to let go of the old stories and attachments to the past and feelings of shame, anger, regret, and pain. You decide how you wish to move forward to create the life you want to have right now.

FORGIVE TO LIVE

Take a moment to reflect on a past situation or event that continues to leave you feeling angry, hurt, resentful, bitter, and demanding justice. Then, when you're ready, close your eyes and bring the event to mind. What happened? Who did the wrong—you or someone else? How were you or others hurt? What didn't you get then that you are longing for now? Allow yourself several minutes with these questions.

- Step 1: awareness. Become aware of the pain you feel about that past event. Allow yourself to experience it as it is. Where does it hurt now? See if you can face it squarely. What does it feel like? What does it look like? Notice your mind linking your pain with judgment, blame, and negative evaluations.

- Step 2: separation. Use your observer self to separate the judgment from the pain you're having now. Notice judgment as judgment, blame as blame, and bitterness as bitterness, without engagement. Simply watch and create space between what the mind tells you and your felt experience.

- **Step 3: compassionate witness.** See if you can step back even further, as if you're watching this event play out on a giant movie screen. Imagine being in the audience, simply watching, as though you're someone seeing this drama unfold for the first time. See if you can open up your heart to be a compassionate witness to the actors in this scene. See who's doing the hurting. See who's receiving the hurt. See who's responsible for doing the hurting. See the person responsible for the felt pain, then and now.

- **Step 4: letting go and moving on.** Now kindly ask yourself this: Who's in control over the resentment you feel now? Who's getting hurt, right now, by your holding on to the memory of the past wrong? Who has the power to let go and move on? The answer is you. You can let go of holding on to the wish and hope for a resolution. You can take the energy and effort focused on resolving, fighting back, or getting even and put it to better use. You can bring kindness to your experience by facing your pain squarely for what it is. Own it because it is yours, and then choose to let it go.

If you're willing to let the resentment and rage go, then do that. If you're having trouble doing that, then think about who's getting hurt when you hold on to it. Is it you, or the person who once wronged you? Imagine what you'd do with your mental time and energy if you were no longer consumed by resentment and recycled rage. What would you think about instead? What would you feel? What would you do? Take time with this.

Remember, this practice is for you, not for people or circumstances that once hurt you!

46 The Gift of Gratitude

Imagine there was one simple quality you could use to cultivate inner peace and genuine happiness. Wouldn't that be something? Well, there is one. It's called gratitude.

Science teaches us that the practice of being grateful for what we have has enormous benefits. It improves health. Relationships. Well-being. Even sleep. It improves our emotions too, allowing us to feel more positive feelings and to bounce back from stress and difficulty. It can also give a powerful boost to self-esteem. So people who practice gratitude on a daily basis end up happier and healthier, and they live longer than those who focus on what they don't have, or are missing.

But don't expect to notice dramatic changes overnight. Cultivating gratitude is a skill and requires time and practice. To reap the full benefits of gratitude, it's best to commit to it on a daily basis. The good news is, you have everything you need to start right now. In fact, we know from research that keeping a gratitude journal for just five minutes a day can boost your happiness by about 10 percent. A study in the journal *Emotion* also showed that this is about the same boost in happiness you'd get if your salary just doubled. That's pretty impressive.

The next journaling exercise will help you build gratitude into your daily life.

GRATITUDE JOURNAL

For the next two weeks, keep a gratitude journal. Before going to bed, take a moment to reflect on the day, and then write down up to five things for which you feel grateful. The physical record is important—don't just do this exercise in your head. The things you list can seem relatively trivial ("The tasty sandwich I had for lunch today" or "Having toilet paper in the bathroom") or quite significant ("My sister gave birth to a healthy baby boy" or "I was able to do something that's important to me even when I felt anxious").

The goal of the exercise is to recognize an event, experience, person, or thing in your life that you can be grateful for—then enjoy the good emotions that come with it. See the good things in your life as "gifts" rather than taking them for granted. Some of the things you realize you are grateful for may surprise you—savor these! Allow yourself ten to fifteen minutes to do this each day for at least two weeks.

There are only three guidelines to follow here.

1. **Be specific.** This is the key to fostering gratitude. Writing "I am grateful that my partner brought me soup when I was sick today" is better than "I am grateful for my husband."

2. **No duplication, at least for two weeks.** Each day you must look for some new things to be grateful for. It can be as simple as being grateful for that cup of coffee at breakfast, having soap to wash with, or making time to meditate.

3. **Pause and reflect.** Before you wrap up your daily entry, pause and reflect on what you've just written down. See if you can connect with your heart and with a deeper sense of appreciation for what you have.

You can certainly keep journaling well beyond two weeks if you'd like to. But eventually you'll want to consciously practice appreciation and gratitude in the moment, wherever you find yourself during your day. As you do, be specific about what you have to be grateful for in your life. Sink into the sweetness of that.

The ultimate purpose of the journaling is to heighten your conscious awareness of what you have to be grateful for. If you start paying attention to all these glimpses of gratitude that your heart shows you, you'll notice them more often and more clearly.

Gratitude is also closely related to happiness. If you experience, and sometimes also express, your gratitude, you will feel happier. More gratitude equals more happiness, and here we mean more than happiness "the feeling." We're talking about a deeper and more lasting sense of contentment and joy. So if you want to experience greater genuine happiness in your life, then becoming more grateful for what you have is an easy and effective way to start.

47 Paying It Forward

Every time you perform a kind act for others, you stand to get a boost yourself. Studies are clear on this point. People who get into the habit of performing kind actions, large and small, are happier and healthier. And it's not that they're happier people to begin with, which might explain why they're so giving. It turns out that the very act of performing an act of kindness leaves us feeling good. When we give, we get a sense of satisfaction and pleasure. You've probably heard it said, "If you want to be happy, make other people happy." Kindness and compassion not only produce greater happiness, but they also loop back to give us a sense of deeper purpose and connection to others.

Kindness has many other benefits. When you are feeling disempowered, even trapped in anxiety and fear, the very act of doing something kind for others can leave you feeling empowered. In times of weakness, acts of kindness are really acts of strength.

But don't be kind just to get something from someone else in return. This is not about getting accolades, appreciation, or gushing thanks from other people. You do a kindness "just because"—say, because it's good for you to do it, or it's something only you can do. But when you give kindness expecting to get something in return, you will often end up disappointed.

When you practice kindness "just because," you break free from expectation and can sink into the goodness of what you and you alone can do. This, in turn, can often create a ripple effect. When you act kindly toward others, including yourself, the act pays itself forward: other people are more likely to act in kind ways too.

Practicing kindness toward others, let alone toward ourselves, does not come easily for many. Doing so may even feel contrived at first. But don't let that stop you. The next exercise will help you to build this life-affirming practice into your daily life.

PRACTICE ACTS OF KINDNESS

Start by making an intention to act kindly toward yourself and toward others. You don't need to wait to feel peaceful and loving before you decide to act in a kind and loving way. You can just do it regardless of what and how you feel. Here are some ways to get started.

- Practice saying "Please," "Thank you," and "You're welcome" more often. You might open a door for someone, offer a helping hand, extend a smile to a stranger, or let a

driver merge into traffic. Give a hug or a kiss
to a loved one. Show understanding, compassion, and forgiveness when you feel hurt and
get the urge to strike back.

- Look for moments when you can share what
  you have—talents, interests, time, resources,
  a meal.

- Watch for times when you can show care and
  moments when you can offer gratitude or
  extend warmth.

- Look for times when you can offer hope, love,
  or a helping hand. Do this when you'd rather
  shut down, tune out, or explode.

With practice, acts of kindness will become automatic
and leave you with a deepening sense of peace, love, and
trust. Regardless of the target or the outcome, kindness is
fundamentally about you! Nurture it. Develop it. Make it
the core of your being and how you choose to live. Pay kindness forward, and it will loop back to you in positive ways.

48 Taking the Reins

We are each the master of our own destiny. Nobody else can create your life for you. Blaming others or your anxiety for keeping you stuck won't help you either. You have to decide that enough is enough. There is no undoing your past or making it go away. So ask yourself how you want to live your life from this moment forward. To be successful, you'll need to be clear about where you have a voice and a choice.

Life is about choices—and you have full responsibility for the choices you make. Coming to terms with this can feel both sobering and liberating. However, deep down you know that you cannot *choose* whether or not to feel panic, anxiety, or worry. If anxiety were a choice, then nobody would choose to feel it.

With LIVE the choice is to practice a more inviting and welcoming relationship with your anxiety. Instead of choosing to treat it as an enemy, you can learn to treat it as a friend. This doesn't mean that you like everything about anxiety, any more than you like everything about a friend, partner, or family member. But you have a good deal of say in *how you choose to respond* to your emotional upset and pain when you feel it—and *what you do* with it.

MAKING DIFFERENT CHOICES

Let's take a look at some specific situations in which you have the power to choose what you do when your anxieties and fears show up:

- I can observe what my mind says without further action, rather than doing what my mind says.

- I can meet my anxieties with compassion and allow them to be there, rather than struggling with them or trying to make them go away.

- I can observe what my body does, rather than listening to what my mind tells me about what my body does.

- I can do nothing about the anxious feelings and thoughts, rather than distracting myself, taking pills, and running away from them.

- I can practice patience with myself, rather than blaming and putting myself or others down for having anxieties.

- I can move forward in my life with anxieties, rather than struggling with them and remaining stuck.

It's your choice whether you stay with your anxieties, acknowledge their presence, let them be, and observe them with a sense of curiosity and kind acceptance, or do as they say, pick up the rope in the tug-of-war, and give in to the impulses to act by choosing avoidance, escape, suppression, or other ways to try to control or get rid of them. It really is your choice.

49 Inhabiting Your Body

Just as you can touch the armrest of a chair, feeling its texture, so too can you make contact with your emotional life. The practice is to get to know yourself and what it's really like to feel what you feel when anxiety and fear show up.

So the practice is to touch your experience, make room for it, and learn something new. But remember, this isn't about wading in the muck and discomfort for its own sake. This is not about white-knuckling it either. The practice is to open up to what your body and mind offer. No more resisting or struggling. In this way, you transform your relationship with yourself and create the space you need to move in directions you truly care about.

As you practice the next exercise, remember why you're doing it. This is about living your life with anxiety or without anxiety. No more fighting. No more resisting. You open up, with compassion and curiosity, to your emotional experiences. This opening up is probably the kindest thing you can do for yourself.

EMOTIONAL CONTACT

Start by getting yourself comfortable in a place where you'll be undisturbed for five to ten minutes. Follow the instructions as best you can and use your imagination to bring them to life in your mind and heart.

- What is hardest for you about feeling anxiety or fear? Pause for a moment and think about what you feel in your body, focusing on your physical sensations. What physical sensations do you typically experience (for example, tension, racing heart, dizziness, nausea)?

- How do these physical sensations tend to get in the way of what you want to do? Here, focus on something important to you—one of your important values.

- Now stop. Pick one of the physical sensations that you would be willing to explore.

- For that one physical sensation, decide if you're willing to explore it as it is. Remember, willingness is a choice—you choose it or not. Unless you're willing, there is no point in moving on. So decide if your life and your values are important enough that you'd be willing to see what it's really like to feel what you feel.

- Now ask yourself, "Did I feel this one physical sensation before it was part of my anxiety?" Look deeply into your past, because you probably did feel it. As you look back, ask yourself, "Must this one physical sensation really be my enemy?" And even if you don't like it, are you willing to have it just as it is— one physical sensation in your body?

- Now close your eyes and focus on that important value of yours. See yourself doing what you care about as that one physical sensation shows up.

- Notice the sensation in your body with some curiosity. Where do you feel it? What is it really like? Now breathe spaciousness and kindness into and out of that physical sensation. Imagine touching it with the breath of healing and kindness. Continue until you sense some spaciousness.

- Now again consider that one physical sensation. Is it really your enemy? Or can you hold it gently when it shows up, and go ahead and do what you care about? You can, even if your mind tells you no!

- Before finishing, pause and think about what you learned about yourself. You are learning to inhabit your emotional body in a new way.

This exercise may have been hard to do, but it will get easier with practice. In that spirit, allow yourself time to repeat this exercise several times, sticking with only one physical sensation. Do that until you truly begin to sense some space to hold that sensation without resistance or struggle. Then you can move on to another sensation that you're willing to explore. As you do, be mindful that you're changing your relationship with your emotional body. No longer fighting, you're in a place where you can move with it and do what you care about in your daily life. You are now the one in charge!

50 Growing Through Adversity

Anxiety and your other emotional pain and hurt are not your enemies. They are your teachers. Think about that for a moment. Without experiencing disappointment, you'd never learn to hold your expectations about the future more lightly. Without the hurt and frustration, you'd never learn kindness and compassion or perseverance. Without exposure to new information, you'd never learn anything new. Without fear, you'd never learn courage. Even getting sick once serves a purpose—it strengthens your immune system and helps you to appreciate good health.

Moments of adversity and pain provide you with opportunities for growth and change. They teach you important skills. They give you new perspectives on life. You need them. They offer you great opportunities to expand beyond your comfort zone and thrive.

When you face difficulty, focus on what you can control to have your needs met and to keep you moving forward in directions that you care about. When you have painful experiences, apply your compassionate observer skills to them. Choose to open up to and embrace them in the service of doing something you care about. This is something you can do.

But you'll need a specific plan that keeps you moving forward even in the face of adversity. You'll need to be able to catch the old unhelpful programming so you can create the conditions for genuine happiness to grow within you. The next exercise will help you on this path.

GOING BACKWARD OR FORWARD?

Whenever you encounter barriers and you're unsure whether your planned action is good for you, ask yourself one simple question: "Is my response to this event, thought, feeling, worry, or bodily sensation moving me closer to or further away from where I want to go with my life?" The following are some variations of this crucial question:

- If that thought (emotion, bodily state, memory) could give advice, would the advice point me forward in my life or keep me stuck?

- What advice would my value _____ [bring to mind a core value of yours] give me right now?

- What would I advise my child or someone else to do in this situation?

- If others could see what I'm doing now, would they see me doing things that I value?

- In what valued direction have my feet taken me when I listened to this advice?

- What does my experience tell me about this solution? And what do I trust more—my mind and feelings, or my experience?

When you face adversity and doubt, it is far more helpful to ask questions like these than to listen to what your unwise anxious mind comes up with or what the surging impulses seem to be telling you. The answers will remind you that past solutions have not worked. Now you can choose to do something new.

51 One Step at a Time

Your life is made up of the steps you take—what you do. Each and every step will move you either toward or away from what matters to you. The key is to step wisely, for with these steps you create your life and the conditions for genuine happiness.

Wise steps are those guided by your values—your North Stars that we talked about earlier. Values, as you learned, act like a beacon. They point you toward what's important to you. This is crucial when you feel pulled and pushed around in a sea of worry, anxiety, panic, and doom and gloom.

The wonderful thing about values is that they can give a very personal meaning to your life. The key to living out your values is, again, to break them down into incremental steps. Living a rich life is all about taking steps, however small or large, toward achieving your goals and living your values, each and every day.

You must commit to taking those steps. You do that by setting SMART goals and following through with action.

Let's go over the elements of SMART goals, one by one:

1. Specific—Identify concrete goals on your path.

2. **M**eaningful—Set goals that matter to you and reflect your values.

3. **A**ctive—Select goals that you can accomplish yourself and that add to your life satisfaction and vitality in some way.

4. **R**ealistic—Set goals that are reasonable, given your life circumstances.

5. **T**ime-framed—Be able to make a commitment to the day and time when you plan to take the step, and the setting. (And after you complete a step, don't forget to pat yourself on the back!)

SMART goals are like destinations that you'll visit in your journey toward living out your values—stepping-stones along your valued path. Now it's your turn.

The next exercise will teach you how to set SMART goals that embody your values and move you in directions that truly matter to you.

CREATING SMART GOALS

Select a value that you wish to manifest more fully and wholeheartedly in your life. Write it down in a word or two and keep it in mind as you develop SMART goals that bring that value to life in your life.

Once you have this value clearly in mind, close your eyes, and ask yourself, "What would others see me doing that would be an outward expression of this value?" Think as small or as large as you wish, but be specific. Keep the image of what you saw yourself doing clear in your mind. If you like, you can also jot it down. You now have a Specific goal.

Next, listening to your heart and what you really care about and want to be about as a person, ask yourself, "Does this really matter to me? And does this action express my heart?" If you answer yes, then you have a Meaningful goal.

Look again at your specific goal. Be sure it's something you can control and do with your mouth, hands, and feet. And be sure it's something that could leave you with a sense of satisfaction and vitality, even if doing what you're setting out to do may at times be challenging. An active goal ought to be something that gets your mouth, hands, and feet moving and has the potential to leave you with a sense that you just did something good for yourself and your life. If you think that's true of the action you selected, then you have an Active goal.

Is the goal Realistic and does it have a doable Time-frame? Here it's important to look honestly at your life and circumstances. Ask yourself whether you may need to coordinate your plans with others. And don't set a goal that is fanciful or beyond what you can do. Walking three times a week for twenty minutes may be a realistic SMART goal in the service of values related to health, or even values linked to being out in nature. But suddenly deciding to run a marathon tomorrow may be unrealistic.

The last important piece here involves action in your life. Once you set a SMART goal, take the step to live out your values in situations that have been difficult for you. Make a commitment and follow through. Use all the tools in this book to help you move with your anxious mind and body. Then give yourself time to reflect on what you've learned and what it felt like to do something good for yourself and your life.

Don't be discouraged if now and then you fail to take the step. When that happens, come back to what's important, recommit to your SMART goal (or even adjust it as needed), use the skills in this book, and then commit to taking another step once more. Even baby steps will take you up the tallest of mountains.

52 The Journey Ahead

You've probably heard the saying "Life's a journey, not a destination." However trite it may be, it contains a great truth. No matter how you look at it, your journey—everything you spend your time doing or not doing—is what you'll look back on someday and call your life.

You deserve to be genuinely happy. And your journey isn't over yet. Along the way, you'll face new obstacles, doubts, and setbacks. The old anxiety barriers will show up too. At times, you won't put your commitments into action. Sometimes you'll slip into old anxiety habits. Once in a while, you may take longer to reach a goal than you had hoped. All of this and more is just fine. We each move at our own pace.

You can draw upon the strategies and skills you've learned in this book when *difficulty* threatens to get in the way of *vitality*. This is how you keep yourself moving forward and LIVE!

Sitting still with your anxieties, doubts, and fears and not getting all tangled up with them is one of the toughest parts when practicing courage on a day-to-day basis, and so is the first step of LIVE: letting go of the internal dialogue and struggle. Over time, you'll get more skilled—so long as you keep practicing kindness toward your own slipups, limitations, and all-too-human inability to be perfect.

Begin each day with this commitment. Perhaps it's something like "Today, to the best of my ability, I'm going to act with kindness and courage." Then follow that with an intention to make your day a value-rich day. In the evening, go back and examine your day with loving-kindness. Don't beat yourself up if your day ends up being filled with some of the same old things you've always done. Look for the new and vital things you did do that day.

Compassion, softness, flexibility, and courage are skills and powerful antidotes to suffering. Recognize that you're only human and that you're going to make mistakes and experience setbacks. You're never going to be able to be courageous and accepting all the time; still, you keep moving in directions you care about, one day at a time.

What matters is that you are taking steps to bring acceptance and compassion to yourself and your worries, anxieties, and fears. The small steps eventually add up. Sooner or later you'll find that kindness and patience have become habits in your life. Give yourself time. Working through this book in the span of several weeks is not the end of something. It's the beginning of a new chapter in your life. And the work isn't over with this book. Your life journey takes a lifetime.

Keep practicing the skills you've learned in this book. Focus on exercises and metaphors that have been especially helpful in getting you unstuck and moving forward. Revisit them and focus on them.

Finally, many of the exercises in this book include forms of meditation. There is a good reason for this. Based on our own experience and countless research studies, we know that meditation is one of the most powerful ways to bring greater happiness and fulfillment to your life. The Dalai Lama once said that if every child going to school today would learn meditation and practice it, there would be peace in the world twenty years from now. Even if you're much older than a five-year-old, it's never too late to make changes and create peace, at least in your own life. So choose a meditation that works for you and stick with it. You won't regret it.

It's risky to make changes. Things sometimes do go wrong or don't turn out as intended. Yet the biggest risk in life is taking no risk at all. Few things in life are certain. The future is, by definition, unknowable. Most choices involve risk for this very reason. Choosing to play it supersafe guarantees that nothing will change. And if nothing changes, you'll end up going where you've always headed before—a place where you're stuck, suffering, and waiting for your life to begin. Risking living your life, while you can, is risky business, but the payoff is huge—you'll get more of what you want. When you risk living out your dreams, those dreams just might come true.

Before we wrap up, let's take a moment to reflect on a question that you can apply again and again throughout your life. This is not an exercise that you just do a few times and then move on. Instead, it is a very practical and fundamental practice that we encourage you to keep on doing for the rest of your life—an approach to LIVE your life.

LIVE THE LIFE QUESTION

What we call the "life question" is by far the single most important question life is asking you when you're faced with barriers, problems, and pain.

At those times, *stop*, take a deep breath or two, and ask yourself this simple life question:

Am I willing to take all that life offers and still do what matters to me?

We all need to face this question squarely and be willing to answer it, moment by moment, for as long as we're alive.

And it turns out that yes is the only answer that will help you create a life in line with your values. To answer no means only one thing: you're choosing not to live the life you want. Even if you find yourself answering no to the life you want right now, remember, you can always choose to change your answer, to take a bold step on a new path, and to risk doing something new to get a different outcome in your life.

The most rewarding thing you can do to create a life that matters is to put each moment of every day to good use. How you decide to use your precious time and energy from this day forward is up to you. Anxiety happens to everyone. But you don't have to let it take over and control your life. You can focus on making your life happen. The skills you've been learning in this book are your friends to help you stay on track, anxiety or not.

Use your time wisely. There's no going back, no way to carry over to tomorrow the lost moments of today. In the end, it all adds up to what you'll call your life. Make the most of it. Make it about something bigger than your anxiety. We know you can do it. You have the skills. Continue to nurture them. Allow them to grow. Make your values a reality. This is what matters and what, in the end, leads people to say, "Now there was a life well lived."

John P. Forsyth, PhD, is professor of psychology and director of the anxiety disorders research program at the University at Albany, SUNY. Forsyth is a highly sought-after speaker, acceptance and commitment therapy (ACT) workshop leader, and member of the teaching faculty at the Omega Institute for Holistic Studies, the Esalen Institute, and 1440 Multiversity. His teachings and writing focus on how to use ACT and mindfulness practices to alleviate suffering, awaken the human spirit, and cultivate well-being. He is coauthor of *The Mindfulness and Acceptance Workbook for Anxiety*.

Hulse Photography LLC

Georg H. Eifert, PhD, is professor emeritus of psychology and former associate dean of the School of Health and Life Sciences at Chapman University in Orange, CA. Eifert is an internationally recognized author, scientist, speaker, and trainer in the use of ACT. He is coauthor of *The Mindfulness and Acceptance Workbook for Anxiety* and *The Anorexia Workbook*.

Forsyth and **Eifert** are also coauthors of *Acceptance and Commitment Therapy for Anxiety Disorders* and, with Matthew McKay, *ACT on Life Not on Anger* and *Your Life on Purpose*.